INVESTMENT MANAGEMENT

Securities and Portfolio Management

INVESTMENT MANAGEMENT

Securities and Portfolio Management

B. Hiriyappa

PUBLISHING FOR ONE WORLD

NEW AGE INTERNATIONAL (P) LIMITED, PUBLISHERS

New Delhi • Bangalore • Chennai • Cochin • Guwahati • Hyderabad
Jalandhar • Kolkata • Lucknow • Mumbai • Ranchi

Visit us at **www.newagepublishers.com**

Published by New Age International (P) Ltd., Publishers
First Edition: 2008

ISBN (10): 81-224-2256-X

ISBN (13): 978-81-224-2256-6

Rs. 160.00

C-07-11-2088

Printed in India at Nisha Enterprises, Delhi.
Typeset at Inhouse.

PUBLISHING FOR ONE WORLD

NEW AGE INTERNATIONAL (P) LIMITED, PUBLISHERS
4835/24, Ansari Road, Daryaganj, New Delhi - 110002
Visit us at **www.newagepublishers.com**

Dedicated

To

My Noble Mother

PREFACE

"Investment Management is the process of managing money, including investments, budgeting, banking and taxes, also called as money management". "An Investment operation is one which, upon through analysis promises safety of principal and an adequate return. Operations not meeting these requirements are speculative".

It is sincerely hoped that the book will be useful to the Investors, CEO, Directors, Managing Directors, Strategy Planner, Students and Faculty Members of BBM, MBA, MCOM, PGDM, PGDBM, PGDHRM, ICFAI and competitive examinations in India and abroad. I invite suggestions from one and all for improvements in next edition of this book.

Investment management has been introduced as a subject in BBM, MBA, MCOM, PGDM, PGDBM and ICFAI. I have made humble effort to fulfill the needs of the Investor, Planner, CEO, Directors of MNCs, Students and Teachers of the subject by covering necessary topics, explaining ,analysis and assessing the various aspects and subjects.

Many individuals have rendered their helping hand to me. I take this opportunity to thank all of them. I thank Dr. D.M. Basavaraja, my teacher, guide and supervisor and professor from Kuvempu University for his constant inspiration and support, Dr. C.M. Thagaraju, Dr. G.T. Govindappa, my teachers, and professors of Kuvempu University. I am immensely indebted them. I also thank T.N. Suresh, Director of Padmashree group of institutions, Bangalore, Dr. C.N. Aswath Narayan, Chairman of Padmashree group of institutions. Bangalore, Dr. A.Venkta Raju, Professor, ATNCC, Shimoga, Prof. Sheshchalla, KKECS, Bangalore, Chairman, Principal, HOD and staff of the T. John Institute of Management and Science.

Shri Saumya Gupta, MD, and Shri. Sudarshan. S.P., Marketing Manager, Chief Editor, Manager and Staff, the New Age

International (P) Ltd. Publisher, these persons are the main initiators and monitors of this project. I express my sincere gratitude to all of them.

It is my prime responsibility to thank my parents, brother, sisters and friends for inconveniences caused during writing of this book.

DR. B. HIRIYAPPA

CONTENTS

CHAPTER

1

INVESTMENT

Learning Objectives

- What is investment, speculation and gambling.
- Explain the different modes of investment for investor.
- Discuss the financial investments, physical investments, maketable investments and non marketable investments.
- What are the factors influencing the investment?
- Who is investor? What are the qualities of investor? Discuss the different types of investor.

INTRODUCTION

"An investment operation is one which, upon thorough analysis promises safety of principal and an adequate return. Operations not meeting these requirements are speculative."

- By Graham and Qadd's Security Analysis

"Investment Management is the process of managing money, including investments, budgeting, banking and taxes, also called as money management."

We shall discuss about the following factors:

- Firstly: Meaning, concept, characteristics, need and importance, avenues, classification and modes of investment.
- Secondly: Influencing factors, process, feature, source of risk, recent trends and problems of investment.
- Thirdly: Meaning, characteristics, difference in speculation, investment and gambling.

MEANING AND CONCEPT OF INVESTMENT

Investment is a term for several closely related meanings in finance and economics.

Investment according to Theoretical Economics

Investment means the production of capital goods - goods which are not consumed but instead used in future production.

Examples include

- Building
- A rail road
- A Factory clearing land
- Putting oneself through college

Investment according to Finance Term

Investment means buying of Assets. For Examples

- Buying stocks and bonds
- Investing in real estate
- Mortgages

These investments may then provide a future income and increase in value (*i.e.,* investing in real estate).

Investment according to Oxford Dictionary

Investment means the investing of money.

Investment from an Individual Point of View

Investment refers to a money commitment of some sort. For example

1. A commitment of money to buy a new car is certainly an "investment".

CHARACTERISTICS OF INVESTMENT

Investment refers to invest money in Financial physical assets and Marketable assets. Major investments features such as risk, return, safety, liquidity, marketability concealability, capital growth, purchasing power, stability and the benefits.

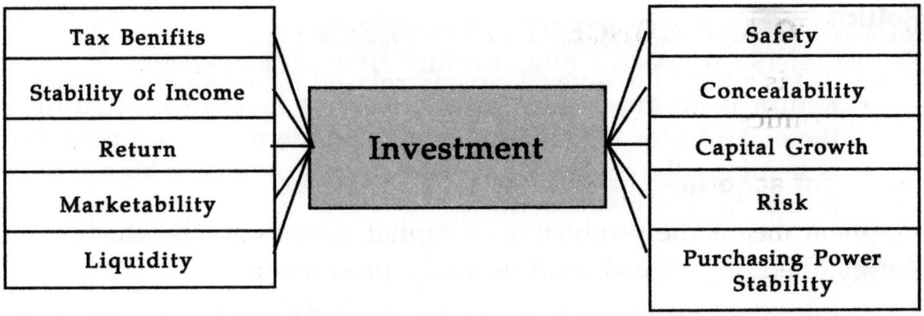

Fig. 1.1 Characteristics of Investment

Figure 1.1 indicates that an important characteristics of investments is outlined as:

- Risk
- Return
- Safety
- Liquidity
- Marketability
- Concealability
- Capital growth
- Purchasing power stability
- Stability of income
- Tax benefits.

Risk

Risk refers to the loss of principal amount of an investment. It is one of the major characteristics of an investment.

The risk depends on the following factors:

- The investment maturity period is longer, in this case, investor will take larger risk.
- Government or Semi Government bodies are issuing securities which have less risk.
- In the case of the debt instrument or fixed deposit, the risk of above investment is less due to their secured and fixed interest payable on them. For instance Debentures.
- In the case of ownership instrument like equity or preference shares, the risk is more due to their unsecured nature and variability of their return and ownership character.
- The risk of degree of variability of returns is more in the case of ownership capital compare to debt capital.
- The tax provisions would influence the return of risk.

Return

Return refers to expected rate of return from an investment

- Return is an important characteristics of investment. Return is the major factor which influences the pattern of investment that is made by the investor. Investor always prefers to high rate of return for his investment.

Safety

Safety refers to the protection of investor principal amount and expected rate of return.

- Safety is also one of the essential and crucial elements of investment. Investor prefers safety about his capital. Capital is the certainty of return without loss of money or it will take time to retain it. If investor prefers less risk securities, he chooses Government bonds. In the case, investor prefers high rate of return investor will choose private Securities and Safety of these securities is low.

Liquidity

Liquidity refers to an investment ready to convert into cash position. In other words, it is available immediately in cash form. Liquidity means that investment is easily realisable, saleable or marketable. When the liquidity is high, then the return may be low. For example, UTI units.

An investor generally prefers liquidity for his investments, safety of funds through a minimum risk and maximisation of return from an investment.

Marketability

Marketability refers to buying and selling of Securities in market. Marketability means transferability or saleability of an asset. Securities are listed in a stock market which are more easily marketable than which are not listed. Public Limited Companies shares are more easily transferable than those of private limited companies.

Concealability

Concealability is another essential characteristic of the investment. Concealability means investment to be safe from social disorders, government confiscations or unacceptable levels of taxation, property must be concealable and leave no record of income received from its use or sale. Gold and precious stones have long been esteemed for these purposes, because they combine high value with small bulk and are readily transferable.

Capital Growth

Capital Growth refers to appreciation of investment. Capital growth has today become an important character of investment. It is recognising in connection between corporation and industry growth and very large capital growth. Investors and their advisers are constantly seeking 'growth stock' in the right industry and bought at the right time.

Purchasing Power Stability

It refers to the buying capacity of investment in market. Purchasing power stability has become one of the import traits of investment. Investment always involves the commitment of current funds with the objective of receiving greater amounts of future funds.

Stability of Income

It refers to constant return from an investment. Another major characteristic feature of the Investment is the stability of income. Stability of income must look for different path just as security of principal. Every investor always considers stability of monetary income and stability of purchasing power of income.

Tax Benefits

Tax benefits is the last characteristic feature of the investment. Tax benefits refer to plan an investment programme without regard to one's status may be costly to the investor. There are actually two problems:

- One concerned with the amount of income paid by the investment.
- Another is the burden of income tax upon that income.

NEED AND IMPORTANCE OF INVESTMENTS

An investment is an important and useful factor in the context of present day conditions. Some factors are important. They are as outlined below:

- Longer life expectancy or planning for retirement
- Increasing rates of taxation
- High interest rates
- High rate of inflation
- Larger incomes
- Availability of a **complex number** of investment outlets.

Longer Life Expectancy

Investment decisions have become more significant as most people in India retire between the ages of 56 to 60. So that, they are planned to save their money. Saving by themselves do not increase wealth, saving must be invested in such a way that the principal and income will be adequate for a greater number of retirement years.

Longer life expectancy is one reason for effective saving and further investment activity that help for investment decisions.

Increasing Rates of Taxation

When tax rate is increased, it will focus for generating saving by tax payer. When the tax payer invest their income into provident fund, pension fund, Unit Trust of India, Life Insurance, Unit Linked Insurance Plan, National Saving Certificates, Development Bonds, Post Office Cumulative Deposit Schemes etc. It affects the taxable income.

Interest Rates

Interest rate is one of the most important aspects of a sound investment plan. The interest rate differs from one investment to another. There may be changes between degree of risk and safe investments. They may also differ due to different benefit schemes offered by the institutions.

A high rate of interest may not be the only factor favouring the outlet for investment. Stability of interest is an important aspect of receiving a high rate of interest.

Inflation

Inflation has become a continuous problem. It affects in terms of rising prices. Several problems are associated and coupled with a falling standard of living. Therefore, investor careful scrutiny of the inflation will make further investment process delayed. Investor ensures to check up safety of the principal amount, security of the investment. Both are crucial from the point of view of the interest gained from the investments.

Income

Income is another important element of the investment. When government provides jobs to the unemployed persons in the country, the ultimate result is ensuring of income than saving the extra income. More incomes and more avenues of investment have led to the ability and willingness of working people to save and invest their funds.

Investment Channels

The growth and development of the country leading to greater economic prosperity has led to the introduction of a vast areas of investment outlets. Investment channels means an investor is willing to invest in several instruments like corporate stock, provident fund, life insurance, fixed deposits in the corporate sector and unit trust schemes.

INVESTMENT ACTIVITY

Investment activity includes buying and selling of the financial assets, physical assets and marketable assets in primary and secondary markets. Investment activity involves the use of funds or savings for further creation of assets or acquisition of existing assets.

Figure 1.2 indicates the investments activity. Accordingly investment activity refers to acquisition of assets like:

- Financial Assets
- Physical Assets
- Marketable Assets from the Primary and Secondary Market

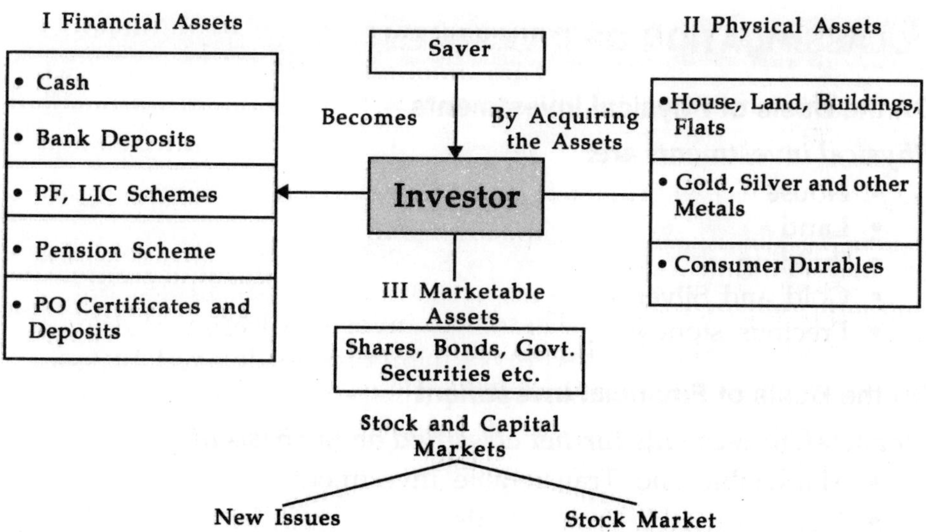

Fig. 1.2 Investment Activity

Financial Assets are:

- Cash
- Bank Deposits

- P.F.
- LIC Schemes
- Pension Scheme
- Post Office Certificates and Deposits

Physical Assets are:

- House, Land, Building and Flats
- Gold, Silver and other Metals
- Consumer Durables

Marketable Assets are:

- Shares
- Bonds
- Government Securities
- M.F. Schemes
- UTI Units etc.

Investment activity involves the use of funds or savings for further creation of assets or acquisition of existing assets.

CLASSIFICATION OF INVESTMENT

On the Basis of Physical Investments

Physical investments are:

- House
- Land
- Building
- Gold and Silver
- Precious stones

On the Basis of Financial Investment

Financial investments further classified on the basis of:

- Marketable and Transferable investments
- Non-Marketable Investments

Marketable and Transferable Investments

Marketable investments are:

- Shares
- Debentures of Public Limited Companies, particularly the listed company in Stock Exchange

- Bonds of Public Sector Units
- Government Securities, etc.

Non-Marketable Investments

Non-marketable investments are:

- Bank Deposits
- Provident and Pension Funds
- Insurance Certificates
- Post office Deposits
- National Saving Certificates
- Company Deposits
- Private Companies Shares etc.

MODES OF INVESTMENT

Modes of investment consist of:

- Security Forms of Investment
- Non-Security Forms of Investment/Non-Marketable Investment

Security Forms of Investment

Security forms of investment includes the following:

- Corporate Bonds/Debenture
  - (a) Convertible
  - (b) Non-Convertible
- Public Sector Bonds
  - (a) Taxable
  - (b) Tax Free
- Preference Shares
- Equity Shares
  - (a) New Issue
  - (b) Rights Issue
  - (c) Bonus Issue

Non-Security Forms of Investment (non transferable)

Non-security forms of investment as outlined below:

- National Savings Scheme
- National Savings Certificates

- Provident Funds
  - (a) Statutory Provident Fund
  - (b) Recognised Provident Fund
  - (c) Unrecognised Provident Fund
  - (d) Public Provident Fund
- Corporate fixed deposits
  - (a) Public Sector
  - (b) Private Sector
- Life insurance policies
  - (a) Whole Life Policies
  - (b) Limited-payment Life Policy
  - (c) Convertible Whole Life Assurance Policy
  - (d) Endowment Assurance Policy
  - (e) Jeevan Mitra
  - (f) The Special Endowment Plan with Profits
  - (g) Jeevan Saathi
  - (h) The New Money Back Plan
  - (i) Marriage Endowment/Educational Annuity Plan with Profits
  - (j) Bima Sandesh Premium Back Term Insurance Plan
  - (k) New Children's Deferred Assurance Plan
  - (l) Jeevan Dhara
  - (m) New Jana Raksha Plan with Profits
  - (n) Jeevan Akshay Plan
  - (o) Jeevan Balya Plan
  - (p) Jeevan Kishor
  - (q) Jeevan Griha
  - (r) Jeevan Sarita and Others
- Unit schemes of Unit Trust of India (Some are marketable among these)
  - (a) Unit Scheme, 1964
  - (b) Reinvestment Plan, 1966
  - (c) Unit Linked Insurance Plan, 1971
  - (d) Capital Gains Unit Scheme, 1983
  - (e) Children's Gift Growth Funds, 1986
  - (f) Parent's Gift Growth Funds, 1987

(g) Monthly Income Unit Scheme with Extra Bonus Plus Growth
(h) Master Shares
(i) Master Gains
(j) Equity Linked Savings Scheme
(k) Growing Monthly Income Unit Scheme
(l) Mastershare Plus etc.

- Post Office Savings Bank Account
  (a) Recurring Deposits
  (b) Time Deposits
  (c) Monthly Income Scheme
  (d) Social Security Certificates
- Others
  (a) Rahat Patras or Relief Bonds
  (b) Kisan Vikas Patra
  (c) Deposits in Co-operative Banks
    (i) Recurring deposits
    (ii) Time deposits, etc.

INVESTMENT FOR CONSUMPTION AND BUSINESS

The income is divided into two components, namely:

- Consumption
- Investment

The income which is not consumed is saved and invested. Investments are also useful for present and future consumption in the case of consumer durables, cars, gold and silver etc. But investment generally promote larger consumption in future as they lead to more income and larger capital appreciation in the years to come.

Some investments in business are used in trade and transport and other services. Thus, doctors, lawyers, traders etc. spend money for making investments for their business, which lead to further consumption of income.

Importance of Financial and Physical Investment

Many savers will have their first preference for physical investments which are less productive and rarely income earning. Such investments are in consumer goods like, non-durables or durables, gold, silver, cars and antiques and 'curios'. These are satisfying the immediate consumer needs, for comfort, luxuries, social status, ego buildings etc. Some of them if rented out to others give income and sometimes capital appreciation also, if the location is at the good places or commercial areas. Similarly, gold, silver and other metals, diamonds and antiques may present capital appreciation, without giving any regular income. Some investments are for social status and prestige as gold, diamonds, jewelry etc.

FACTORS INFLUENCING INVESTMENT

Investment refers to investment of physical assets, financial assets and marketable assets. Legal safe guards, stable currency, existence of financial institutions to encourage savings and forms of business organization factors are influenced to investor to invest money in different investment avenues.

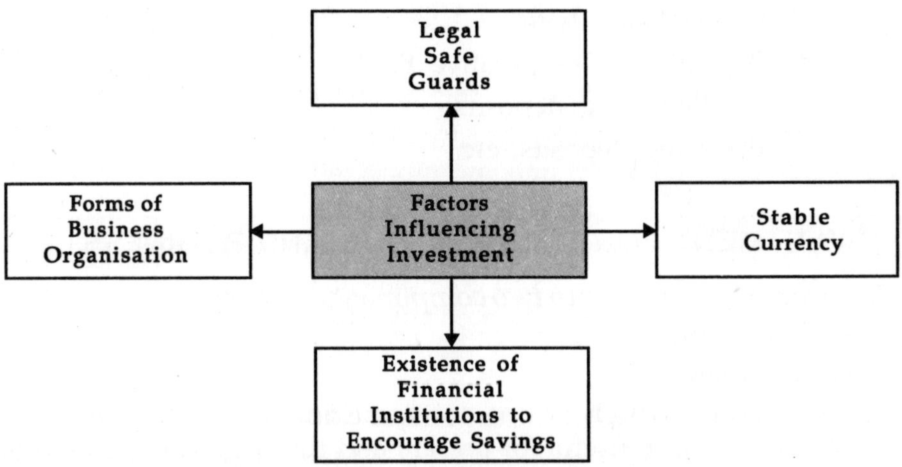

Fig.1.3 Factors Influencing Investment

Figure 1.3 shows the influencing factors of investment, as outlined:

- Legal safeguards
- Stable currency
- Existence of financial institutions to encourage savings
- Form of business organisation

Legal Safeguards

A stable government brings adequate legal safeguards that encourages accumulation of savings and investments. Investors will be willing to invest their funds. They want the assurance and protection of their property rights from the government.

In India, the investors have the dual advantage.

- Free enterprise
- Government control

India is a mixed economy. It encourages the combination of the public sector which is controlled by the government and private sector left free to operate with a hope to achieve the benefits of both socialistic and capitalist forms of government without any disadvantages.

A Stable Currency

A well organised monetary system with definite planning and proper policies is a necessary pre-requisite to an investment market. Most of investments in terms of bank deposits, life insurance and shares are payable in a fixed amount of the currency of the country. A proper and well organised monetary policy will give direction to the investment outlets. Therefore, the monetary policy should neither promote acute inflationary pressures nor prepare for a deflation model. Neither of them is desirable. It affects as:

- Price inflation destroys the purchasing power of investments.
- Deflation is equally disastrous because the nominal values of inventories, plant and machinery and land and building tend to shrink.

The wise and planned monetary and fiscal management contributes towards proper control, good governance, economic well being and a well disciplined growth-oriented investment market along with the protection to the investor.

Existence of Financial Institutions to Encourage Savings

Existence of Financial Institutions which encourage savings and directing them effective utilisation of investment through growth of investment market. The financial institutions are generally in existence in most countries in terms of

- Commercial Banks
- Life Insurance Companies
- Investment Companies.

In India, the presence of large number of financial institutions under Central Government and local bodies have encouraged the growth of savings and investment. Life Insurance Corporation and Unit Trust of India offer a wide variety of schemes for savings and give tax benefits also.

- Industrial Development Bank of India (IDBI)
- Industrial Credit Investment Corporation of India (ICICI)
- Industrial Finance Corporation of India (IFCI)
- State Financial Corporations
- National Bank of Agriculture and Rural Development (NABARD)
- Commercial Banks
- Co-operative Banks
- Life Insurance Corporation
- Unit Trust of India
- Development Banks

These financial institutions offer wide variety of policies for encouraging savings and investment.

FORMS OF BUSINESS ORGANISATION

- Company
- Sole Trading Concern
- Partnership Firms
- HUF

These are different forms of business organisation. The form of business organisation which is permanently in existence aides saving and investment. The public limited companies is the best form of business organisation for investment.

The public limited companies are very useful to investors because of the following reasons:

- Limited Liability of Shareholders
- Perpetual Life and Transferability
- Divisibility of Stock and Shares
- The Ability to Continue its Business Irrespective of Members Comprising it
- It gives longevity and soundness to business activity.

In the case of sole trading concern, partnership and Hindu undivided family systems are not useful to investors because of the following reasons:

- Unlimited liability of the owners, partners and members.
- It suffers short life of the organisation.

In such conditions investors are not ready for investment because there is no safety and security of their investment.

The public limited company is popular form for investment. The following reasons are attracted to investors to invest in public limited Companies. They are:

- Liquidity
- Convenience
- Longevity
- Stable return.

THE INVESTMENT PROCESS/STAGES

Investment process refers to investment policy, investment analysis, valuation of securities and proper portfolio construction in this way achieve to investment process.

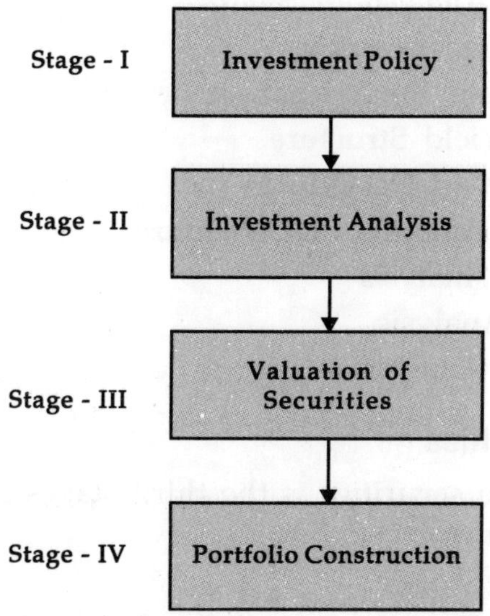

Fig. 1.4 The Investment Process/Stages

Figure 1.4 indicates the investment process/stages. The investment process/stages are outlined below:

- Investment Policy
- Investment Analysis
- Valuation of Securities
- Portfolio Construction

Investment Policy

Investment policy is the first stage of the investment process. It determines the following aspects of the investor:

- Determination of Investable Wealth
- Determination of Portfolio Objectives
- Identification of Potential Investment Assets
- Consideration of Attributes of Investment Assets
- Allocation of Wealth to Asset Categories.

Investment Analysis

Investment analysis is the second stage of the investment process. Investor analysis of the investment is made on the following grounds:

- Equity Stock Analysis
- Screening of Industries
- Analysis of Industries
- Quantitative Analysis of Stocks
- Analysis of the Economy
- Debentures and Bond Analysis
- Analysis of Yield Structure
- Consideration of Debentures
- Quantitative Analysis of Debentures
- Other Asset Analysis
- Qualitative Analysis
- Quantitative Analysis

Valuation of Securities

Valuation of the securities is the third stages of the investment process. This stage involves

- Valuation of Stocks
- Valuation of Debentures and Bonds
- Valuation of Other Assets

Portfolio Construction

Portfolio construction is the last stage of the investment process. It involves the following areas as outlined below that:

- Determination of Diversification Level
- Consideration of Investment Timing
- Selection of Investment Assets
- Allocation of Investable Wealth to Investment Assets
- Evaluation of Portfolio for Feedback

Features of an Investment Programme

Exhibit 1.1 Features of an Investment Programme

Features of an investment programme consist of the following factors:

- Safety of principal amount
- Liquidity of the investment
- Income stability of the investment
- Appreciation and purchasing power stability of the investor investment
- Legality and freedom from care about the investment
- Tangibility of the investment

SOURCES OF INVESTMENT RISK

According to the Oxford dictionary definition of risk includes the following meanings: "The possibility of meeting danger or of suffering harm or loss." This conforms to the connotations put on the term by most investors. An investor commonly identifies five kinds of investment risks. They are:

- Business and Financial Risk
- Interest Rate Risk
- Purchasing Power Risk
- Social/Regulatory Risk
- Other Risk

Business and Financial Risk

Business risk and financial risk are actually two separate types of risks. Of course, they are interrelated. Business risk is also known as operating risk. Operating risk is associated with day to day operations of the business firm. Financial risk is created by debt and preference shares (Fixed cost securities). Business and financial risk may be caused by a variety of factors as mention below:

- Heightened Competition
- Emergence of New Technologies
- Development of Substitute Products
- Shifts in Consumer Preferences
- Inadequate Supply of Essential Inputs
- Changes in Government Policies
- Poor Business Performance.

Interest Rate Risk

Interest rate risk is another source of investment risk. Changes of the interest rates on the securities is created risk for investors. If the interest rate goes up, the marketing price of existing fixed income securities falls, and vice versa. This happens because the buyer of a fixed income security would not buy if its par value or face value if its fixed interest rate is lower than the prevailing interest rate on a similar security.

Market Risk

Even in the case of earning power of the corporate sector and the interest rate structure remain more or less changed, prices of securities, equity shares in particular, tend to fluctuate. There are several reasons for this fluctuation.

The main reasons are listed below:

- The changing psychology of the investors.
- There are periods when investors become bullish and their investment horizons lengthen.
- An unexpected war, the election year, political activity, illness or death of an important person, speculative activity in the market, the outflow of business-all are tremendous psychologic factors in the market.

These reasons result in that the prices of almost all equity shares register decline as fear and uncertainty spread in the market.

Purchasing Power Risk

Purchasing power risk is the major source of risk faced by investors. The investor select investments whose market values change with consumer prices which compensates them for increase in cost of living. If they do not, they will find that their total wealth has been diminished. Inflation which destroys the economic power of investors over goods and services. In essence, all investors have to be concerned with the command that their invested money has over goods and services on a continuing basis.

Other Risks

Other types of risks are particularly associated with investment in foreign securities. It involves monetary value risk and political environment risk. The investors who invest in foreign securities, have faced several risks. They are outlined as below:

- A change in the foreign government and repudiation of outstanding debt

- Nationalisation of business, firms, that is, seizure by government
- The desire but inability of the foreign government or corporation to handle its indebtedness.

RECENT TRENDS OF INVESTMENTS

Exhibit 1.2 Recent Trends of Investments

Recent trends of investments are

- In India, increase in working population, larger family income and consequent higher savings
- Provision of tax incentives in respect of investments in specified channels provided by government
- Increasing tendency of people to hedge against inflation that protected by government
- Availability of large and attractive investment alternatives developed in India
- Increase in investment related publicity in India
- Ability to invest to get income and capital gains etc.

PROBLEMS IN INVESTMENT

Exhibit 1.3 Problems in Investment

- Inadequate comprehension of return and risk
- Investment policy is not clearly formulated
- Careless decision making in investment process
- Simultaneously switching of investment activity
- Traditional trends affected to the investment
- Inadequate planning to buy cheap stocks
- Either over diversification or underdiversification of stock
- Investors are ready to buying shares of familiar companies that problem for investment in future
- Wrong attitude towards losses and profits
- Tendency and difficult to speculate to investments

SPECULATION

According to the Oxford Dictionary, definition of speculation includes the following meanings:

"A message expressing an opinion based on incomplete evidence."

Speculation is the buying, holding and selling of stocks commodities, collectibles real estate or any valuable thing to profit from fluctuations in its price as opposed to buying it to use. Sometimes speculative purchasing can cause particular prices to rise above their "real value" simply because the speculative purchasing is artificially increasing the demand. Speculative selling can also cause prices to fall below "true value" in a similar fashion. In some situations price rises due to speculative purchasing cause further speculative purchasing in the hope that the price will continue to rise.

Speculation Functions

Exhibit 1.4 Speculation Functions

- Smoothen operating of price fluctuation process
- It maintains temporary equilibrium between capital supply and demand
- Consideration of future business prospects in determining the business value of existing capital funds
- Equating the risk to return in the infinitely varied utilisations of the social capital fund

Difference between Speculation and Investment

Basis	*Speculation*	*Investment*
Meaning	• A message expressing an opinion based on incomplete evidence	• The investing of money
Types of contract	• Speculator is a owner of the speculation	• Investor is a creditor of the Investment
Length commitment	• In the case speculation the length of commitment is a short term only	• In the case of investment the length of commitment is a long term
Source of Income	• The source of income is fluctuated and changes in market price	• The source of income is earning from the enterprise
Quantity of Risk	• Quantity of risk is the high	• Quantity of risk is the low
Stability of Income	• Income is uncertain and erratic	• Income is very stable
Psychological attitude of Participants	• Speculator psychological attitude is a daring and careless	• Investor psychological attitude is a cautious and conservative
Reasons for Purchase	• It is unscientific analysis of intrinsic worth	• It is scientific analysis of intrinsic worth

Difference between Investor and Speculator

Exhibit 1.5 Differene between Investor and Speculator

Base	*Investor*	*Speculator*
• Planning Horizon	• An investor has a relatively longer planning horizon. His holding period is usually at least one year	• A speculator has a very short planning horizon. His holding may be a few to a days to a few months
• Risk Disposition	• An investor risk is less	• A speculator risk is high
• Return Expectation	• An investor usually seeks moderate rate of return	• A speculator looks for a high rate of return
• Basis for Decisions	• An investor attaches greater significance to fundamental factors and attempts a careful evaluation of the growth of the enterprise	• A speculator relies more on hear say, technical charts and market psychology
• Leverage	• An investor uses his own funds avoid borrowed funds	• A speculator normally takes to borrowings, which can be very substantial, to supplement his personal resources.

GAMBLING

According to the Oxford dictionary, gambling means:

"Taken risk in the hope of a favourable outcome." Gambling most often refers specifically to the wagering of money on games of chance or more broadly to engaging in high risk behaviour. Gambling refers to an act of involving an element of risk. A gambling involves taking on risk without demanding compensation in the form of increased expected return.

Characteristics of Gambling

Exhibit 1.6 Characterlstics of Gambling

An important characteristics of gambling

- Gambling is a typical, chronic and repetitive experience
- Gambling absorbs all other interests
- The Gambler displays persistent optimism without winning
- The gambler never steps while wining
- The gambler eventually take more risk
- The gambler seeks and enjoys a strange thrill from gambling
- The gambler seeks pleasure and pain from gambling
- In gambling artificial and unnecessary risks are created

The Position

Many investors are tax paying individuals. The income tax rates vary from 10% to 30%. The tax rate on capital gains of a long term lower at 20%. While the short term capital gains are taxable at slab income tax rates. Long term capital gain and short term capital gain depends on the nature of investments. In the case the investments in terms of corporate shares and securities that holding for more than 12 months by the investor will make them as long term nature. While other investments like as house, land, gold etc. that holding for more than 36 months by the investor will make them as long term nature. If shares and securities holding by the investor less than 12 months. And house, land, gold which holding by the investor less than 36 months will make them as short term capital gain.

Specialised Knowledge

In investment management, there is need for a sort of expertise. Therefore, investment is both a science and an art. If the return on investment is high, the degree of risk is also high with expected returns and time frame investments. Time is an important element for both tax purposes and for risk taken.

Specialised knowledge, effective and proper management of investment involves:

- Efficient use of cash and proper distribution of money among different investments channels.
- Proper analysis of risk and return for each investments
- Expertising analysing information in terms of technical analysis and security analysis for proper investment decisions that are based on a study of fundamentals, expectations and mood of the markets.

Thus, the investment management involves various elements for getting best returns in the form.

- Study of tax implications
- Time duration and proper strategy for reducing taxes and increasing the after tax returns
- Excellent knowledge for understanding financial markets.

INVESTOR

"A person whose principal concern in the purchase of a security is the minimizing of risk, compared to the speculator who is prepared to accept calculated risk in the hope of making better-than-average profits, or the 'gambler' who is prepared to take even greater risks. More generally it refers to people who invest money in investment products."

"An individual who makes investments. An investor can act on behalf of others, for example, stock brokers or mutual fund managers make investments for others. Or else an investor can make investments for ones own personal account."

Qualities of Investor

- **Safety Players**

  Safety Players who take the path of least resistance, looking primarily for security and safety in their investments and doing what has worked previously.

- **Entrepreneurs**

  Entrepreneurs are a particularly male-dominated profile driven by a passion for excellence and commitment, and who are not motivated by money in itself. Financial success is a scorecard and stock investment is a method of implementing and demonstrating that success.

- **Optimists**

  Optimists are non-risk oriented, often near retirement, seeking peace of mind, these are investors who don't like to become too involved with their own financial management as it would cause them stress and reduce their enjoyment of life.

- **Hunters**

  Hunters are often educated, high-earning women with an impulsive streak, a 'live now attitude.' They have a strong work ethic, much like entrepreneurs, but lack the same confidence in themselves. They may attribute their success to luck rather than ability.

- **Achievers**

  Achievers are conservative, risk-averse, these investors like to feel in control of their money, with security and protection of their assets a primary consideration. They are often, married, well educated, high-earners who feel that hard work and diligence is more likely to bring financial reward than investing.

- **Perfectionists**

  Perfectionists are afraid of making financial mistakes, they tend to avoid investment decisions altogether. They lack confidence and self-esteem, and have low pride in handling financial matters, finding every conceivable excuse for not taking action. For them no investment is without fault.

- **Producers**

  Producers are highly committed to their work. They may earn less due to a lack of self-confidence in money management. And with a lack of basic financial knowledge they may have less available funds to invest. They do not appreciate how to evaluate risk appropriately.

- **High Rollers**

  High Rollers are thrill seekers, power seekers, creative and extroverted, they work hard and play hard. They have to be involved in high risk investing with a large amount of their assets. Financial security bores them - even though their actions may have financially dangerous consequences.

- **Money Masters**

  Money Masters are tending to have a balanced financial outlook that gives contentment and security, these investors like to be involved with the management of their money and their choice of investments, although they will take onboard good, sound advice. They are determined individuals, not easily thrown of their chosen course, and who don't leave things to luck.

- **Adventurers**

  Adventurers are confident 'go for it' types who are strong-willed and ready to take chances.

- **Celebrities**

  Celebrities are those who need to be in the center of things and don't like to be left out, often constantly checking whether they should be in the latest fashionable investment but may not really have any clue as to how to take control of their finances.

- **Individualists**

  Individualists are confident individuals who make their own decisions but who are methodical, careful, balanced and analytical.

- **Guardians**

  Guardians are investors, often older ones, who are cautious and intent on safeguarding their wealth, shunning volatility or excitement.

- **Straight arrows**

  Straight arrows are Mr. or Mrs. Average who do not fall into any of the extremes of the above categories, who is somewhat balanced in their investment approach and willing to take on moderate risk.

Types of Investor

- **Cautious Investors**

  Cautious Investors are very conservative, this type of investor has a need for financial security and will avoid high-risk ventures as well as listening to professional advice, preferring to conduct their own financial affairs. They don't like to lose even small amounts of money and never rush into investments, always giving financial opportunities a great deal of thought.

- **Emotional Investors**

  Emotional Investors are easily attracted to fashionable investments or 'hot' tips, these investors act with their heart and not their head. A whim or a gut feeling leads their decisions, and they have great difficulty disengaging from poor investments or cutting losses. They have an unreasonable belief that things will come right in the end and often put their trust in luck or 'providence' to safeguard their financial assets.

- **Technical Investors**

  Technical Investors are hard facts - numbers - lead this type of investor to active trading based on price movements. They are screen-watchers, sometimes obsessional, but their diligence can be rewarded if they spot trends. They may also have a tendency to 'need' and buy the latest technology as they are always looking for some edge.

- **Busy Investors**

  Busy Investors need to be involved with the markets, it gives them a *buzz* when they check the latest price movements, which may be several times a day. They have to keep buying and selling - on rumours, on overheard gossip, from the mass of newspapers and magazines they collect. Any tidbit of information they can glean is imbued with significance and a cause to take financial action.

- **Casual Investors**

  Casual Investors are a laid-back attitude to investment, these individuals are often hardworking and involved with work or family. They tend to believe that once an investment is made it will take care of itself, and that a good job or a profession is the way to make real money. They easily forget that they own investment assets and rarely check on their financial affairs. And, though they may leave the running of their investments to professional advisors, they haven't been in contact with them for years.

- **Informed Investors**

  Informed Investors use information from a variety of sources and keep an ongoing watch on their investments, the markets and the economy. They listen carefully to financial opinions and expert assessments, and will only go against market fashion, as a contrarian, after weighing up all the pros and cons. They are financially confident and have faith in their decisions, knowing that knowledge and experience will always win out to give them long-term profits.

- **Passive Investors -**

  Passive Investors are characterised as individuals who have become wealthy passively - by inheriting, by a professional career or by risking the money of others rather than their own money. To these investors security is more important than risk. In addition, certain classes of occupation are more likely to contain passive investors. For example, non-surgical doctors, corporate executives, lawyers and accountants who work in companies. Reasons for this are that these individuals are less likely to have high financial resources at an early stage in their careers, having had to delay earning good salaries in order to study or having to repay student loans. Once earning a decent wage, they are then more careful with their money, having a greater need for security. Anyone, therefore, with reduced financial recourses is likely to be more risk conscious and hence, a passive investor. For these individuals it's important to hang on to their money.

  Passive investors make good clients because they tend to trust their financial advisor and are more likely to delegate the running of their financial affairs. And because they are risk averse, they tend to like diversified portfolios of investments in quality companies or investment products. However, they can believe that an investment is more risky than it is, which may keep them out of potentially lucrative opportunities. Passive investors are also more likely to need the approval of others and are unlikely to take a first step into unknown investment territory by being a contrarian. Consequently, they are more likely to follow the investment herd when it comes to stock market investment and stick to following the trend.

- **Active Investors**

  According to Barnwell, Active Investors are those who have achieved significant wealth, or earned well, during their own lifetime. They are more likely to take risks in investing because they have previous experience of taking risks in their previous wealth creation. These individuals have a high-risk tolerance and less of a need for security. They also need to feel in control of their own abilities. Once they feel they are losing control of an investment situation, their risk tolerance reduces. By being actively involved and in control, these investors *feel* they are reducing risk. However, such involvement may actually be detrimental as it is likely to be a source of irritation to their investment advisor who cannot get on with the business of running their clients affairs due to constant questioning and harassment. The classes of occupation that are likely to be active investors include: small business owners who have developed their own businesses rather than inherited, medical surgeons, independent professionals, such as lawyers or accountants, who work for themselves rather than a large firm, entrepreneurs, and self-employed consultants.

  Active investors are more likely to get personally involved with the running of their financial affairs, and may believe they know more than their advisor does. They are less likely to delegate the maintenance of those parts of their investment portfolio in which they believe they have experience or have had personal success. However, these individuals are more likely to be contrarian in their stock picking habits and have less need to be completely diversified. Age tends to soften their need to be constantly in control, so that older clients may be more malleable and open to their advisors suggestions.

QUESTIONS FOR DISCUSSIONS

1. Define term investments.
2. Outline the reasons for the emerging popularity of today's investment world.
3. Define the term speculation.
4. Define the term gambling.
5. Discuss the characteristics of investment.
6. Discuss the characteristics of investors.

7. What is investment activity?
8. What are the difference between investment and speculation?
9. What are the difference between investor and speculator?
10. Discuss the most common problems observed in analysing investments of individual investors.
11. Discuss the feature of investment programme.
12. Describe the concept of investment.
13. What are the importance of investments?
14. Discuss the terms:
    - Financial investments
    - Physical investments
    - Marketable investments
    - Non-marketable investment
15. Discuss the classification of investment.
16. Describe the modes of investment.
17. Explain what are the objectives of investment?
18. Why do people invest? What are the factors which are favourable for making decisions in investments in an economy?
19. Describe the features of an investment programme? What steps should an investor follow to make an investments?
20. What are characteristics of gambling?
21. Discuss the process of investment.

REFERENCES

Stevenson, Jennings, *Fundamentals of Investments,* West Publishing House, New York, 1977.

Dougall, Herbeat, E., *Investments,* 9th ed., Prentice Hall, Englewood, N.J., 1978.

Amling, Frederick, *Investments* 3rd ed., Prentice Hall, Englewood, N.J. 1978.

Smith, Eiteman, *Modern strategy for Successful Investing,* Dow Jones Irwin Inc., Illinois, 1978.

Fischer and Jordan, *Security Analysis and Portfolio Managements,* Prentice Hall.

Prasanna Chandra, *Investment Analysis and Portfolio Management,* Tata McGrow Hill, 2003.

Fabozzi, F., and I.M. Pollach, *The Hand Book of Fixed Income Securities,* 2nd ed. Homewood., III.: Dow Jones Irwin, 1987.

Bhole, L.M., *Financial institutions and Makets,* Tata McGraw Hill, New Delhi, 2003.

Khan, M.Y., *Indian Financial Management System: Theory and Practice.*

Farrell, J.L., Jr., *Portfolio Management,* Second edition, McGraw Hill, New York, 1997.

Jones, C.P., *Investments: Analysis and Management,* Second Edition, John Wiley and Gon, New York, 1988.

Brealey, R.A., *An Introduction to Risk and Return on Common Stocks,* Cambridge, Mass, MIT Press, 1969.

Brown, R., *"Risk and return is Emerging markets"* Investing/Spring 1991.

Prasanna Chandra, *Financial Management,* Tata McGraw Hill, New Delhi, 2004.

I.M. Pandey, *Financial Management,* Vikas Publishing House, 2004.

Bhalla, V.K., *Investment Management,* S. Chand and Co. Ltd., New Delhi, 1982.

Fredrick Amling, *Investments: An Introduction to Analysis and Investment,* Engle-wood Cliffa, N.J. Prentice Hall, 1978.

Clark Francis J., *Investment Analysis and Management,* McGraw Hill, 2nd ed. U.S.A., 1976.

■■■

CHAPTER

2

FINANCIAL ARITHMETICS

Learning Objectives

- We shall know the interest: simple interest and compound interest.
- We shall understand the annuity and its associated terms.
- Describe the concept and types of Yield.
- Explain the yield calculations.
- What is the time value of money ? Give the reasons of time preference money.
- What is the importance of time value money.
- Discuss the techniques of discounting.

INTRODUCTION

In this Chapter, we shall discuss about the interest, simple interest, annuity and its terms, concept and types of yield or return, yield rate, bond/coupon rate, holding period yield, realised and expected yield, current yield, redemption yield, dividend yield, earning yield, gross and net yield, time value of money, reason for time preference money, preference for present consumption, importance of time value of money, technique of compounding and technique of discounting.

INTEREST

Interest is the payment of extra money made by a borrower for having used the money lent by others for certain period of time. If Rama borrows Rs. 10,000 from Krishna for one year. Rama has to pay back Rs. 10,000 plus some extra amount as a consideration for having used Krishna's money. The extra payment made is known as interest. The money actually borrowed is called as principal and the total sum consisting principal and interest is called the amount, interest is always calculated for certain period at a specified rate.

SIMPLE INTEREST

Simple interest is the interest always calculated on the principal. It is assumed that simple interest is paid at the end of a specified period regularly. Even if the interest is not paid regularly, it does not get accumulated for the calculation of further interest. For instance, Rs. 10,000 is borrowed at 10% p.a. naturally at the end of first year the simple interest works out to Rs. 1,000. Even if it is not actually paid, the interest for the next year is computed only on the original principal borrowed and never the accrued interest is added with the principal for further calculation of interest. So, simple interest for 5 years works out to Rs. 5,000, *i.e.*, Rs. 1,000×5.

The formula for calculating simple interest is

$$SI = Pni$$

where,

P stands for principal

n stands for number of years (period)

i stands for rate of interest per unit

By using above formula, the following formula can be obtained:

Total amount = Principal (1 + ni);

$$A = P(1+ni)$$

Simple interest (SI) = Pni

Principal (P) $= \dfrac{SI}{ni}$

Period 'n' $= \dfrac{SI}{Pi}$

Rate of interest per unit, $i = \dfrac{SI}{Pn}$

(Note: Normally 'n' is represented in terms of years; days or months are covered into years).

Problem 1

Find simple interest on

(i) Rs. 1,600 for one year at 10% p.a.

(ii) Rs. 2,500 for 15 months at 15% p.a.

(iii) Rs. 10,000 for 73 days at 20% p.a.

(iv) Rs. 20,000 for one year, three months and 15 days at 24% p.a.

Solution:

(i) P = Rs. 1,600; n = One year; i = 0.10 per unit

$$\therefore \quad SI = Pni = 1600 \times 1 \times 0.10 = \text{Rs. } 160$$

(ii) P = Rs. 2,500; $n = \frac{15}{12}$ years; i = 0.15 per unit

$$SI = 2500 \times \frac{15}{12} \times 0.15 = \text{Rs. } 468.75$$

(iii) P = Rs. 10,000; $n = \frac{73}{365}$ years; i = 0.20 per unit

$$SI = 10000 \times \frac{73}{365} \times 0.20 = \text{Rs. } 400$$

(iv) P = Rs. 20,000; n = 1 year, 3 months, 15 days or 1 year 3½ months.

$$1 \text{ year} + \frac{7}{24} \text{ years or } 1\frac{7}{24} = \frac{31}{24} \text{ years}$$

$$i = 0.24 \text{ per unit}$$

$$SI = 20000 \times \frac{31}{24} \times 0.24 = \text{Rs. } 6{,}200$$

Problem 2

At what rate per cent per annum will

(a) The simple interest on Rs.75 for 9 months be Rs. 4.50?

(b) Simple interest on Rs. 25 for 3 years be Rs. 4.50?

Solution:

(a) SI = Rs. 4.50; P = Rs. 75; n = $\frac{9}{12}$ or ¾ years

I = ?

$$\text{Rate of interest per unit} = \frac{SI}{Pn}$$

$$= \frac{4.50}{(75 \times ¾)}$$

$$= 0.08$$

Rate of interest = 8%.

(b) P = Rs. 25; SI = Rs. 4.50; n = 3 years; I = ?

$$\text{Rate of interest per unit} = \frac{SI}{Pn}$$

$$= \frac{4.50}{(25 \times 3)}$$

$$= \frac{4.50}{75}$$

$$= 0.06$$

Rate of interest = 6%

Problem 3

Find by using appropriate formulae

(a) The amount of Rs. 700 invested for 2½ years at $6\frac{1}{4}$% p.a.

(b) Time in which Rs. 770 will amount to Rs. 847 at 5% p.a

(c) The sum which yields simple interest of Rs. 77 in 8 years at 3½% p.a.

Solution:

(a) P = Rs.700; n = 2.5 years; i = 0.0625; A = ?

ni = 2.5 × 0.0625

Total amount (A) = P(1 + ni)

= 700(1 + 0.15625)

= 700 × 1.15625

= Rs. 809.38

(b) P = Rs. 770; SI = A-P = 847-770 = Rs. 77;

i = 0.05; n = ?

Time(n) = SI + Pi

= 77 + (770 × 0.05)

= 77 + 38.5 = 2 years

(c) SI = Rs. 77; n = 8 years; i = 0.035; P = ?

$$\text{Principal sum (P)} = \frac{\text{SI}}{\text{Pn}}$$

$$= \frac{77}{8 \times 0.035}$$

$$= \frac{77}{(0.28)}$$

= Rs. 275

COMPOUND INTEREST

Compound interest is the interest calculated on the principal and accrued interest. The interest unpaid is added to the principal and for the next period the interest is computed. In other sense, compound interest is the interest on the growing principal. Both principal and compound interest change from time to time. Simple interest is always calculated on the original principal and it is uniformly equal for any period of time. Compound interest changes from period to period since the principal changes. Compound interest can be computed annually, half yearly, quarterly or monthly. The one important fact to be borne is the interest earned on principal is not withdrawn. For instance, on Rs. 1,000, at 10% p.a. interest for one year Rs. 100 and for the second year the principal will be Rs. 1,100 (1000 + 100) and interest for the second year will be Rs. 110. So that compound interest grows since the principal grows.

For compound interest calculation, there are three elements necessary for calculation. They are as below:

- Principal
- Rate per cent
- The period (Time)

The following formulae are kept in mind in solving the problems concerning to compound interest:

$$CI = P(1 + i)^n - P$$

$$A = P(1 + i)^n$$

$$P = A \ (1 - i)^n$$

$P = P(1 + ½)^n$ if CI is paid half yearly and 'n' indicates the number of 'half years' contained in the period.

$$A = P(1 + i/2)^n \text{ etc.}$$

Problem 1

Find compound interest in the following cases:

(a) On Rs. 10,000 for 2 years at 10% p.a. paid annually.

(b) On Rs. 6,000 for 2½ years at 10% p.a. paid annually.

(c) On Rs. 5,000 for 1½ years at 5% p.a., CI is paid half yearly.

(d) On Rs. 1,000 for one year at 10% p.a., CI is paid quarterly.

Solution

(a)

$$P = \text{Rs. } 10{,}000$$

$$n = 2 \text{ years}$$

$$i = 0.10$$

$$A = P(1 + i)^n$$

$$= 10{,}000(1 + 0.10)^2$$

$$= 10{,}000(1.1)^2$$

$$= \text{Rs. } 12{,}100$$

$$CI = A - P = 12{,}100 - 10{,}000 = \text{Rs. } 2{,}100$$

(b) P = Rs. 6,000

$$n = 2\tfrac{1}{2} \text{ years}$$

$$i = 0.10;\ i/2 = 0.05$$

$$A = P(1 + i)^2\ (1 + i/2)$$

$$= 6{,}000(1 + 0.10)^2\ (1 + 0.05)$$

$$= 6{,}000 \times (1.10)^2 \times 1.05$$

$$= \text{Rs. } 7{,}623$$

$$CI = A - P = 7{,}623 - 6{,}000$$

$$= \text{Rs. } 1{,}623$$

(c) P = Rs. 5,000

$$n = 1\tfrac{1}{2} \text{ years or 3 half years}$$

$$i = 0.05; \qquad 1/2 = 0.025$$

$$A = P(1 + i/2)^3 = 5{,}000(1 + 0.025)^3$$
$$= 5{,}000 \times (1.025)^3$$
$$= 5{,}000 \times 1.0769 = \text{Rs. } 5{,}384.45$$
$$CI = A - P$$
$$= 5{,}384.45 - 5{,}000$$
$$= 384.45$$

(d)

$$P = \text{Rs. } 1{,}000$$
$$n = 1 \text{ year or 4 quarters}$$
$$i = 0.10;\ 1/4 = 0.025 \text{ (quarterly)}$$
$$A = P(1 + i/4)^n$$
$$= 1{,}000(1 + 0.025)^4$$
$$= 1{,}000 \times (1.025)^4$$
$$= \text{Rs. } 1{,}103.83$$
$$CI = A - P$$
$$= 1{,}103.83 - 1{,}000$$
$$= \text{Rs. } 103.83$$

ANNUITIES

Annuities means a series of equal payments or receipts accruing over a specified number periods is known as an annuity. The equal payments may be a year, half year, or a quarter or any other period. These periodic payments accumulate at compound interest until the total sum becomes due.

We shall come across a number of schemes for annuity in banks, insurance companies and other commercial establishments. Banks promise to pay a definite amount every month throughout the life time of a person if he deposits a lumpsum in beginning. In case of instalment and hire purchase agreements, the fixation of each instalment associated with interest is done basing on annuity calculation.

The following terms are associated with annuities. The knowledge of which is very crucial.

- Annuity certain
- Immediate annuity
- Annuity due
- Deferred annuity

- Perpetuity and deferred perpetuity.

Annuity Certain

When an annuity is payable unconditionally for a given length of time, it is called annuity certain. It is also known as Life Annuity.

Immediate Annuity

If each of the annuity payment is made at the end of each period, it is called immediate annuity.

Annuity Due

It is an annuity where the first payment falls due in the beginning of the first interval.

Deferred Annuity

It is annuity where the first payment falls due after the lapse of a certain given period which is more than one interval. It is also called reversion.

Perpetuity and Deferred Perpetuity

It is annuity where the payment is to continue for ever, if the payment of annuity is to commence after a certain period, it is known as deferred perpetuity.

Formulae of Annuities

The following formulae are important and helpful in solving problems relating to annuities.

Immediate Annuity

$$A = \frac{P}{i}\left[(1+i)^n - 1\right]$$

Amount of Annuity Due

$$A = P\left(\frac{1+i}{i}\right)\left[(1+i)^n - 1\right]$$

Present value of Deferred Annuity

$$V = \frac{P}{i}\left\{\frac{(1+i)^n - 1}{(1+i)^{m+n}}\right\}$$

where,

V = The present value

P = Annuity

m = The number of years after which the annuity payment has to be commenced

n = The number of years for which the annuity payment is to go.

Present value of Deferred Perpetuity

$$V = \frac{P}{i} \times \frac{1}{(1+i)^m}$$

Present value of Annuity

$$V = \frac{P}{i}\{1 - (1+i)^{-n}\}$$

Present value of Perpetuity

$$V = \frac{P}{i}$$

CONCEPT AND TYPES OF YIELD OR RETURN

The terms of return and yield are mostly used interchangeably. The concept of yield relates on investment made in any security or financial instruments. Yield/return is the amount or rate of produce, proceeds, gain, fruit, profit which accrues to an economic agent from an undertaking or enterprise or (real/financial) investment. It is a reward for and a motivating force behind investment, the main objective of which is usually to maximise return.

Yield/Return on a typical investment has two components. They are as mentioned below:

- The periodic cash or income receipts, wherein terms of interest or dividend

- The appreciation or depreciation in the price or value asset, it is called as the capital gain or the capital loss.

The capital gain (or loss) is the difference between the purchase price of the asset and price at which it can be sold. The income component is usually but not necessary received in cash viz., stock dividend. The total return/yield on an investment thus can be defined as income plus (minus) price appreciation (depreciation).

Yield Rate/Internal Rate of Return

The internal rate of return (IRR) is the rate of discount which makes the present value of all the revenues (cash inflows) from the investment equal to the total cost of that investment. This is also known as the yield or yield rate. The marginal IRR is the rate of discount which makes the present value of the marginal value from the (additional) investment equal to unity.

Bond/Coupon Rate

Bond/coupon rate is the interest rate which received on the face value or the par value of the bond. In the case of a company or the government issues a 10 year bond with Rs.100 as face value and 15 per cent rate of interest. It would be described as 15 per cent bond or debenture and it would be said to have a coupon or bond rate of 15 per cent.

Realised and Expected Return/Yield

Return is not a simple a concept as it appears to be because it is not guaranteed, it should be expected and it may or may not be realised. Hence, the expected return is an anticipated which predicted, desired, ex-ante return and is subject to uncertainty. On the other hand, realised return is actually earned; it is an ex-post return.

Holding Period Yield

Holding period yield measures the total return from an investment during a given or specified time period in which the asset is held by the investor. It is also to be noted that holding period yield does not mean that the securities are actually sold and the gain or loss is actually realised by the investor. The concept of holding period yield is applicable either one is measuring the realised return or estimating the future expected return.

$$\text{The formula of HPY} = \frac{(P_t - P_0) + 1}{P_0}$$

where,

I = Interest payment

P_0 = Price at the beginning of the holding period

P_t = Price at the end of the holding period.

Basic Yield

Basic yield is the lowest return actually attained in the market by high grade bonds of a given maturity and class. This concept is unique and absolutely riskless. It refers absolute safety and certainty of principal and income and also freedom from losses through changes in commodity prices, interest rates, and taxes. The basic yield does not imply either risklessness or uniqueness. It is features on the highest quality bonds.

Current Yield

Current yield refers on investment made in any security or financial instrument. In the case equities, the yield refers to the current yield which means the return on investment made at the presently happening. In the case of debentures and government securities, current yield is the ratio of stated coupon rates per year to the current market price of the bond. It does not take into account the return to be realised by the investor because of the appreciation or depreciation in the value of the bond. It is also known as the market yield or running yield or income yield.

Redemption Yield

Redemption yield is also known as yield to maturity. It is the indicated that the average rate of return involving the return in the form of interest as well as appreciation or depreciation of capital over the period remaining to maturity. Thus,

$$YTM = \frac{(\text{Annual interest}) \pm (\text{Average annual appreciation or depreciation})}{\text{Redemption or Face Value}}$$

Dividend Yield

Dividend yield is the ratio of expected earning per share from investment.

Earnings Yield

Earnings yield is the ratio of expected earnings per share of the firm to the current market price of the share.

Gross and Net Yield

Gross yield refers to the yield realised by the investor before paying taxes. Net yield refers to the yield realised by the investor after paying the taxes. The net of tax yield can be calculated as follows:

$$\text{Net yield} = \text{Gross yield (2-Tax rate)}$$

Required Rate of Return (RRR)

The concept of required rate of return which plays an important role in the valuation of assets and in both financial and real investment decisions. The RRR is defined as the minimum expected rate of return needed to induce or persuade an investor to purchase the security that given its risk.

YIELD CALCULATIONS

Lending of money is for a return in the form of interest. The rates of interest vary with the purpose and maturity and a host of other factors. Hence, advances made by banks and financial institutions are at varying rates of interest and reserve bank has allowed freedom to banks to fix their prime lending rates that are the rates charged for high credit worthy borrowers and the minimum basic rate for lending. In the case of the individuals and institutions make an investment in any asset they base their decision to invest on the basis of some financial arithmetic which takes into account the following factors as below:

- Credit worthiness of the party
- Time period of lending or investment
- Risk of the activity of investments
- Expected returns over the time period choosen
- Safety and marketability of investments.

TIME VALUE OF MONEY

The time value of money means that worth of a rupee received today is different from the worth of a rupee to be received in future. For an individual who behaves rationally a Re. 1 received in future of less valuable than the Re. 1 received today moreover, Re. 1 received two years from now is far less valuable than the Re. 1 received one year from now. This preference for money now, as compared to future money, is called as time preference for money. The concept of time value of money is applicable both for individuals and for business organisations.

REASONS OF TIME PREFERENCE MONEY

An important reasons of time preference money are as outlined below:

- Risk
- Preference for present consumption
- Investment opportunities.

Risk

There is uncertainty about the receipt of money in future. This is the major risk of the investors.

Preference for Present Consumption

Time value of money given preference for present consumption. Most of the persons and companies have a preference for present consumption then future consumption either because of urgency of need. For example, consumer durable or otherwise.

Investment Opportunities

Most of the persons and companies have a preference for present money because of availabilities of opportunities of investment for earning additional cash flows. For example, an individual is offered Rs. 10,000 now or Rs. 10,000 one year later, he would prefer Rs. 10,000 now as he can invest it now and can earn interest on it.

IMPORTANCE OF TIME VALUE OF MONEY

The concept of time value of money involves in arriving at the comparable value of the different rupee amount which is arising at different points of time into equivalent values of a particular point of time either present or future.

The cash flows arising at different periods of time can be made comparable by using any one of the following two ways:

- By compounding the present money to a future date *i.e.,* by finding out the value of the present money.
- By discounting the future money to present date *i.e.,* by finding out present value (PV) of the future money.

TECHNIQUES OF COMPOUNDING

(a) Future Value (FV) of a Single Cash Flow

The future value of a single cash flow is defined as:

$$FV = PV(1 + r)^n$$

where,

FV = Future value n years hence

PV = Present value of cash flow today

r = Rate of interest per annum

n = Number of years for which compounding is done.

(b) Future Value of an Annuity

An annuity is a serious of periodic cash flows either payment or receipt of equal amount. The premium payments of a life insurance policy, for example, are an annuity.

In general terms the future value of an annuity is given as:

$$FVA_n = A\left[\frac{(1+r)^{n-1}}{r}\right]$$

where,

FVA_n = Future value of annuity which has duration of n years

A = Constant periodic flow

r = Interest rate per period

n = Duration of the annuity

From the above mentioned equation it is clear that the future value of annuity is dependent on three variables, *i.e.,* the annual amount, the rate of interest and time period. If any of these variable changes, it will change the future value of the annuity.

TECHNIQUES OF DISCOUNTING

1. Present Value of a Single Cash Flow

The present value of a single cash flow is given as:

$$PV = FV_n\left(\frac{1}{1+r}\right)^n$$

where,

FV_n = Future value n years hence

r = Rate of interest per annum

n = Number of years which discounting is done

The above mentioned formula that present value of a future money depends upon the three variables *i.e.*, FV, the rate of interest and time period.

2. Present Value of an Annuity

Sometimes instead of a single cash flow the cash flows of the same amount is received for a number of years. The present value of an annuity may defined as follows:

$$PVA_n = \frac{A}{(1+r)^1} + \frac{A}{(1+r)^2} + \dots \frac{A}{(1+r)^{n-1}} + \frac{A}{(1+r)^n}$$

$$= \left[\frac{1}{(1+r)^1} + \frac{1}{(1+r)^2} + \dots \frac{1}{(1+r)^{n-1}} + \frac{1}{(1+r)^n}\right]$$

$$= \left[\frac{(1+r)^{n-1}}{r(1+r)^n}\right]$$

where,

PVA_n = Present value of annuity which has duration of n years

A = Constant periodic flow

r = Discount rate

Questions for Discussions

1. Define the following:
   (a) Interest
   (b) Simple interest
   (c) Compound interest
   (d) Annuities
   (e) Annuity certain
   (f) Immediate annuity
   (g) Annuity due
   (h) Perpetuity and deferred perpetuity

(i) The yield

(j) Bond/Coupon rate

(k) Realised and expected return/yield

(l) Holding period yield

(m) Current yield

(n) Redemption yield

(o) Dividend yield

(p) Earning yield

(q) Gross and Net yield

2. Discuss the compound interest and formulae.
3. Explain the annuities and formulae.
4. Briefly explain the concept and types of yield or return.
5. Discuss the time value of money and its techniques.

REFERENCES

Prasanna Chandra, *Financial Management,* Tata McGraw Hill, New Delhi.

I.M. Pandey, *Financial Management,* Vikash Publishing House, New Delhi 2004.

M.Y. Khan and P.K Jain, *Financial Management,* Tata McGraw Hill New Delhi 2000.

James C. Van Home, *Financial Management and Policy,* Prentice Hall of India Pvt. Ltd. New Delhi 2000.

■■■

CHAPTER

3

INVESTMENT OPPORTUNITIES—I

Learning Objectives

- We shall know about the company shares, debentures, fixed deposit companies, Government securities, bonds, post office saving deposits, public provident fund, VIP, money market instruments, bank deposits, precious objects, LIC, real estate, chit funds and mutual funds.

INTRODUCTION

In this chapter, we shall discuss the investment opportunities are:

- Company shares
- Debentures
- Fixed deposit companies
- Government or gilt edged securities
- Bonds
- Post office saving deposits
- Public provident schemes
- Unit trust of india
- Money market instruments
- Bank deposits
- Precious objects
- LIC
- Real estate
- Chit funds
- Mutual funds

MEANING OF INVESTMENT OPPORTUNITIES

Investors are investing their money in company like in terms of equity, preference shares and debentures, fixed deposit in companies, government or gilt edged securities, bonds, post office saving deposits, public provident schemes, Unit Trust of India, bank deposits, LIC, real estate, chit funds, money market instruments, precious objects and mutual funds. These investment avenues is known as investment opportunities.

NON-MARKETABLE FINANCIAL ASSETS

Exhibit 3.1 Non-Marketable Financial Assets

Non-marketable financial assets are listed below:

- Bank Deposits
- Post Office Time Deposits
- Monthly Income Scheme of the Post Office
- Kisan Vikas Patra
- National Saving Certificates
- National Saving Schemes
- Company Deposits
- Employees Provident Fund Schemes
- Public Provident Fund Scheme

Bonds or Fixed Income Securities

Exhibit 3.2 Bonds or Fixed Income Securitites

Bonds or fixed income securities are listed below:

- Government Securities
- RBI Relief Bonds
- Private Sector Debentures
- Public Sector Undertaking Bonds
- Preference Shares

Above are the import bonds or fixed income securities.

EQUITY SHARES

Equity shares are also called common shares and are from the point of view of investment more risky than both bonds and preference shares. Equity capital represents ownership capital. Equity shareholders are real owners of the company. They bear the risk and enjoy the rewards of ownership.

Equity Capital Terminology

An important terms used in equity capital are mentioned below:

- Authorised capital
- Issued capital
- Paidup capital

Authorised Capital: Means "The amount of capital that a company issues as per its memorandum represents the authorised capital."

Issued Capital: Issued capital means that "The amount offered by the company to the investors is called the issued capital.

Paidup Capital: Paid up capital means that "part of the issued capital has been subscribed to buy the investors is called the paid up capital."

Characteristics of Equity Shares

An important characteristics of equity shares as listed below:

- Voting right
- Ownership rights
- Par value
- Right shares
- Tax benefits

Voting rights: This is the fundamental characteristics of the shareholders. Equity shareholders having a special right to cast their vote and elect Board of Directors, Managing Directors in the every annual general meeting.

Ownership rights: This is the second characteristics of the equity shareholders. When investors buy equity shares, they receive ownership certificate *i.e.,* share certificate from particular company where they are invested. When the case equity shares are purchased from the market, the new owner and the number of shares bought are noted in the record book of the transfer agent.

Par value: Par value means the face value of the shares. It indicates from the amount of capital originally subscribed by the shareholders. New shares cannot be sold for less than par value. As regards the equity shares they are sold for more than par, the excess is transferred to "Share Premium Account."

Rights share: The shareholder has a right to receive additional shares when they are issued by the company. Company offeres shares to existing shareholders and then only on their refusal can be offered to others.

Sometimes, some amount is reserved for the existing shareholders and then an issue is made by the company. These right shares are also known as subscription rights. An equity shareholder also receives the right of bonus as well as receiving discount coupons and some times receive more stock in the company in the form of an additional dividend.

Tax benefits: Upto 18,000 can be deducted under Section 80L while computing total income of a person.

Advantages of Equity Share

Exhibit 3.3 Advantage of Equity Shares

The main advantages are listed below:

- Potential Profit

Potential profit and risk of expectation is greater in equity share.

- Limited Liability

The shareholders liability is limited their equity share account. In the case of shareholders may lose their investment, but not their personal investments.

- Hedge Against Inflation

The equity share is a good hedge against inflation.

- Free Transferability

The equity shareholders are free to transfer ownership from one person to another without risk.

- Share in Growth

If a company earns profit, It means that share value has gone up.

- Tax Advantages

Government offers tax advantages to equity shareholders.

Equity Share as an Investment

Exhibit 3.4 Equity Share as an Investment

Equity share is an investment. Its justification of several reasons are outlined below:

- Equity shares are purchased or sale immediately in the stock market and transfer of ownership seller to buyer without delay.
- The liability of the shareholder is limited. Therefore equity share value cannot affect their personal wealth.
- Equity share is taken high risk and high in expected rate of return.
- Equity share earns profit. It means that appreciation to equity share value.

Rights of Equity Shareholders

Exhibit 3.5 Rights of Equity Shareholder

Equity shareholders enjoy the following rights:

- Equity shareholders have a residual claim to the income of the firm. This means that the profit after tax.
- Equity shareholders elect the board of directors and have the right to vote on every resolution placed before the company.
- Equity shareholders enjoy the pre-emptive right and ownership right.
- In the case of income, equity shareholders have a residual claim over the assets of the company in the case of liquidation.

Classification of Equity Shares

Equity shares have been classified on the basis of:

- According to stock market.
- According to Peter Lynch's.

According to Stock Market

Stock market has classified equity shares as follows:

- Blue chip shares
- Growth shares
- Income shares
- Cyclical shares
- Defensive shares
- Speculative shares

Blue chip shares: Blue chip shares means share of large, well established, and financially strong companies shares with an impressive record of earnings and dividends.

Growth shares: Growth shares means shares of companies that have a fairly entrenched position in a growing market and which enjoy an above average rate of growth as well as profitability.

Income shares: Income shares means shares of companies that have fairly stable operations, relatively limited growth opportunities, and high dividend payout ratios.

Cyclical shares: Cyclical shares means shares of companies that have a pronounced cyclicality in their operations.

Defensive shares: Means shares of companies that are relatively unaffected by the ups and downs in general business conditions.

Speculative shares: Speculative shares means shares that tend to fluctuate widely because there is a lot of speculative trading in them.

According to Peter Lynch's Classification of Company Share

Peter Lynch's has classified company shares:

- Slow growers
- Stalwart
- Fast growers
- Cyclicals
- Turn arounds
- Assets plays

Slow growers: Slow growers large and aging companies that are expected to grow slightly faster than the gross national product.

Stalwart: Stalwart giant companies that are faster than slow growers but are not agile climbers.

Fast growers: Small, aggressive new enterprise that grow at 10 to 25 per cent a year.

Cyclicals: Cyclicals companies whose sales and profit rises and fall in a regular, though not completely predictable fashion.

Turn arounds: Turn around companies are steeped in accumulated losses but which show signs of recovery. Turn around companies have the potential to make up lost ground quickly.

Asset plays: Asset plays companies that have valuable assets which have been somewhat overlooked by the stock market.

PREFERENCE SHARES

Preference share is a hybrid security because it combines some of the salient features of debt and some of equity. Preference share has the right to receive its specific dividend before any dividends are paid on the equity. Preference shares usually receives a limited return.

Characteristics of Preference Shares

The salient features of preference shares are as follows:

Dividends: Preference shares carry a fixed rate of dividend. Till recently, the maximum rate of dividend payable on preference shares was 14 per cent per annum. This has now been relaxed.

Redeemable or callable preference shares: Preference shares are redeemable. The redemption period is usually 7 to 12 years.

Right to vote: The preference shareholders in India do not have a right to vote in the annual general meeting of a company and they are entitled for fixed rate of dividend. But in the case non payment of dividend for two or more years in this circumstances the preference shareholder can vote.

Right on assets: The preference shareholders have a similar right to the assets of the company. In the case of liquidation, the preference shares have a prior right to that of the equity shareholders but the payment and the face value of the preference shareholders are paid only after the rights of the bond holders and others creditors are met. Preference shareholders rights will be at last amongst the creditors but before the shareholders.

Par value: The preference shares are usually valued at face value or par value of the preference shares. In India, the preference shares have only a par value. In the case of USA and UK, the preference shares par value is changed at a latter date.

Sinking fund retirement: Preference shareholder usually retired by through creation of the sinking fund. In this case, a certain percentage of earning is allocated for redemption each year. The shares required for sinking fund purposes can be called by lot or purchased in the open market.

Pre-emptive right: The preference shareholders have a right of receiving further issues from the company before it is advertised or offered to other members of the public. In India, the preference shares are not preferred compare to equity shareholders.

Convertible: The preference shares are usually non-convertible unless otherwise stated in a clause inserted at the time of issuing these share. Convertible preference shares means that the owner has the right to exchange a preference share for a share of equity share of the same company. The holder of convertible preference shares usually has a stronger claim than the holder of an equity share to earnings and assets. The convertibility clause gives the preference shareholders a share in the growth of the company. In addition, if a company earning increases, the convertible preference shares will rise in value.

Hybrid: Preference shares is a hybrid security because it combines some of the salient features of debt and some of equity. Therefore, preference shares are considered as Hybrid nature.

Types of Preference Shares

Different types of preference shares are listed below:

- Cumulative or Non-cumulative
- Participating and Non-participating preference shares
- Redeemable and Non-redeemable shares
- Convertible and Non-convertible preference shares

Cumulative or non-cumulative preference shares: Cumulative preference shares have right to receive dividend even if company faces loss to such type of shares is known as cumulative preference shares.

Non-cumulative preference share are one type of preference shares. If company earns profit then will receive dividend otherwise if company is not earning profit, then it will not receive dividend of the same year i.e., Non-cumulative preference shares.

Participating and non-participating preference Shares: Participating preference shareholders can claim to fixed rate of dividend. In addition to entitled to participate in the surplus profits of the company along with the equity shareholders.

Non-participating preference shareholders can claim only fixed rate of dividend. Besides, they are not entitled to participate in the surplus profits of the company along with the equity shareholders.

Redeemable and non-redeemable shares: Redeemable preference shares are those preference shares which can be redeemed or paid back by the company at any time before the company is woundup or after the expiry of a fixed period. These shares can be redeemed only if they are fully paid up. They can be redeemed either out of the profits or out of the fresh issue of shares made for the purpose of redemption. Ofcourse, these shares have preferential right in respect of dividend during the period of their existence.

Non-redeemable shares are those preference shares which can not be redeemed or paid back by the company at any time before the company is wound up. Such shares are known as non-redeemable shares.

Convertible and non-convertible preference shares: Convertible preference shares are those preference shares which can be converted into the equity shares of the company *i.e.,* convertible preference shares.

Non-convertible preference shares are those preference shares which can not be converted into the equity shares of the company *i.e.,* non-convertible preference shares.

DEBENTURES

According to Indian Company's Act, 1956, defined the term 'Debentures.'

Debentures includes debenture stock, bonds and any other securities of a company, whether constituting a charge on the assets of the company or not, in common paralance, debenture is an instrument issued by a company under its common seal, acknowledging its debt to the holder, and containing an undertaking to repay the debt on or after a specified period and to pay interest on the debt at a fixed rate at regular intervals, usually, half yearly, until the debt is repaid.

The person to whom the debentures are issued are called debenture holders. The debenture holders are not the owners of the company. They are just the loan creditors of the company.

Classification of Debentures

Debentures may be classified on the basis of:

- On the basis of transferability point of view
- On the basis of security point of view
- On the basis of priority point of view
- On the basis of period of redemption or repayment
- On the basis of convertibility

On the basis of transferability point of view:

On the basis of transferability point of view, debentures can be classified into two categories, namely:

- Registered debentures
- Bearer debentures or unregistered debentures

Registered debentures: Registered debentures are those in respect of which the names and the addresses of the debenture holders and the particulars of the debentures held by them are entered in the Register of Debenture Holders maintained by the company. *i.e.,* Registered Debentures.

Bearer debentures or unregistered debentures: Bearer debentures are those in respect of which the names and the addresses of the debenture holders and the particulars of the debentures held by them are not entered in the Register of Debenture holders maintained by the company.

On the basis of Security Point of View:

Debentures further classified on the basis of security point of view. They are, namely:

- Simple, naked or unsecured debentures
- Mortgage or secured debentures

Simple, naked or unsecured debentures: Simple debentures are debentures which are not secured by any assets of the company in respect of interest or principal. In this case, the company does not offer any security to the holders either in respect of the payment of interest or the payment of the loan.

Mortgage or secured debentures: Mortgage debentures are debentures which are secured by a charge on the assets of the company. The charge on the assets of the company may be a fixed charge or a floating charge. If the charge is on some specified assets of the company, it is called a fixed charge. On the other hand, if the charge is not on any particular asset of the company, but on the assets in general, it is called a floating charge.

On the basis of Property Point of View:

Debentures may be classified into two types:

- First debentures
- Second debentures

First debentures: First debentures are those which have priority over the other debentures as regarded the repayment of the amount of debentures. In other words, these are debentures which are repaid before other debentures are repaid.

Second debentures: Second debentures are those which are repaid only after the repayment of the first debentures.

On the basis of Period of Redemption or Repayment:

Debentures may be classified into two types namely:

- Redeemable debentures
- Irredeemable debentures

Redeemable debentures: Redeemable debentures are those which are repayable in a lumpsum at the end of a specified period or instalments during the existence of the company.

Irredeemable debentures: Irredeemable debentures are not be repaid. It only means that there is no fixed time for the repayment of these debentures. As such, these debentures are not repaid during the existence of the company. They are repaid only, when the company goes into liquidation.

On the Basis of Convertibility:

There are two types of debentures, namely:

- Convertible debentures
- Non-convertible debentures

Convertible debentures: Convertible debentures are debentures the holders of which are given the option of converting their debentures into shares after a specified period in accordance with terms of conversion given in the prospectus.

Non-convertible debentures: Non-convertible debentures are debentures the holders of which are not given the right to convert their debentures into shares.

FIXED DEPOSITS COMPANIES

The deposits of companies are a form of unsecured loans from the public or promoters and investors of the company. The power to borrow in the form of deposits by companies is vested in the Board of Directors. In terms of the Companies Act. Section 370 deals with inter corporate deposits are also a form of loans but as per companies (Acceptance of

Deposits) Rules, Intercorporate deposits are not considered for the purpose of the limits to total borrowing of the companies. The companies can accept deposits after the resolution passed by the Board of Directors and after giving advertisement in the daily newspapers. Such offer of acceptance of deposits has to be made in terms of the companies acceptance to Deposit rules issued by the department of the company affairs. Such advertisement should also contains the statement of the financial position of the company.

These deposits are unsecured and more risky. The assessment of the risk by the credit rating agency is not compulsory in the case of fixed deposits. As such, the investor has no way of knowing the degree of risk that he is exposed to in contributing to be fixed deposits of the companies. It is made compulsory for NBFCs registered with RBI in 1997.

Terms of Offer of Fixed Deposits

Invitation to deposits from public for various schemes of deposits are invariably published in the news papers in the form of a statutory advertisement which is giving the following details are as below:

- Terms of acceptance of deposits, rate of interest on different maturities, minimum amount of deposits, cumulative or non-cumulative nature of deposits.
- Brief details of the name of the company, date of its incorporation, business carried on by it, places where the company has offices and name and address of the directors.
- Details of profits and dividends for the last three years.
- Summarised financial position of the company (*i.e.*, assets and liabilities) as appearing in the two latest audited balance sheets, along with the details of contingent liabilities.
- Details regarding minimum amount of deposits which that company can accept.
- A specific declaration regarding the deposits accepted are unsecured and would rank pari passu with other unsecured liabilities.
- A statement of deposits remaining unpaid.

Acceptance of Fixed Deposits

A company cannot accept deposits in excess of 35 per cent of its paid up capital and free reserves. Of this, 25% deposits can be accepted from the public and the rest 10% from the shareholders of the company. The minimum period of acceptance of deposits is six months and maximum period is limited to 3 years in the case of nonbank and nonfinancial companies. The maximum rate of interest that can be offered on deposits cannot exceed 15% per annum. A ceiling on brokerage payable on deposits has been fixed at 2%. The interest earned on fixed deposits of companies does not enjoy any exemption from income tax.

The acceptance of deposits by non-bank, nonfinancial companies is governed by the companies (Acceptance of Deposits) Rules 1975 as amended from time to time. Along with the prescribed application form, the terms and conditions of acceptance of deposits are required to be furnished by companies, to the Company Law Board (C.L.B)/Registrar of Companies.

Regulation of Terms of Acceptance

In order to reduce the misuse of powers given to companies to borrow unsecured deposits, the precautions taken by the government are as follows:

- Under Rule 3 of the Acceptance of Deposits Rules, the maximum period is 3 years and a minimum period is 6 months are laid down.
- Maximum interest rate payable is fixed at 15% for a period of three years, but these rates can be varied depending on the credit rating.
- Limits are set on the brokerage to be paid to brokers for securing deposits from the public and would vary from 1 to 2% depending on the period of maturity.
- Limits are set on the total quantum of deposits which can be mobilised from the public.
  - (a) 10% of the aggregate share capital and free reserves as deposits upto six months from directors, shareholders etc.
  - (b) 25% of the paid up capital and free reserves from others, namely, public as deposits above six months.

Complaints Regarding Fixed Deposits

Complaints are arised due to non-payment of principal amounts or non-payment of interest or delays in these respects. Section 58(A) of Companies Act deals with the acceptance of the deposits by the companies. Section 58A(9) has provided for compulsory repayment of maturing deposits. Only, the company Law Board has been empowered to take cognisance of the non-repayment of the deposits or non-payment of the interest on fixed deposits, and action can be taken by the CLB for any complaints of investors.

The following types of deposits do not come in the purview of company Law Board:

- Deposits made for booking purchases of scooter, car etc.
- Deposits accepted by financial companies like hire purchase finance company, a housing finance company, an investment company, a loan/mutual benefit financial company and a chit fund company, which are governed by the rules made by the RBI.
- Deposits accepted by companies which have been notified as 'relief undertakings' under special laws enacted by various State Governments. Court rulings point to the fact that the monetary liabilities of relief undertakings during the notified period stands suspended and any proceedings including the proceedings for compulsory repayment of deposits under Section 58(A)(9) shall accordingly remain stayed.
- Deposits accepted by a sick industrial company covered by the sick Industrial Companies (Special Provisions) Act, 1985 in respect of which, the Board for Industrial and Financial Reconstruction has specifically, by order, suspended the operations of any contract, agreement, settlement, etc., under Section 22(3) of the Act.

Besides, the complaints with regards to fixed deposited of even listed companies cannot be made to the stock exchanges as they have no jurisdiction on them under the listing agreement.

Repayment of Deposits

An additional contingent provision is the obligation of the company to keep 15% of the deposits maturing during the year as a current or other deposit accounts with a Scheduled Bank or in Government Securities to be used only for repayment of deposits to public. This again ensures some safety to investors with regard to repayment, provided for under Rule 3(A) of Acceptance of Deposits rules.

Besides under Sub-section (3A) of Sections 58(A), the company is under an obligation to repay deposits on maturity, unless it is renewed for a further period, a breach of which is an offence and punishable under the Act.

Premature Repayment

Rule 8 of Acceptance of Deposits Rules provided for premature repayment of deposits at the request of depositors, even after a cut in interest rate payable as a penalty.

Issue of Duplicate Certificates

Rules also provide for issue of duplicate receipts after securing Indemnity Bond from the depositor in the event of the certificate. The depositor has to apply to the company in the event of the loss of the certificate and go through the legal formalities for issue of duplicate by the company.

Transmission of Deposits

If a joint holder dies, the amount is payable to survivor. If the investor is a single holder, the transmission of deposit will be as per the will of the deceased or to the legal heirs, in the event of his death intestate (*i.e.*, having made no legally valid will before death).

A succession certificate or probate or letters of administration is called for in these cases. The heirs will have to go to the court having jurisdiction for this. The company may insist on production of an affidavit and an indemnity by the legal heirs or representatives. As the formalities for legal compliance in this respect are cumbersome and time consuming, the investors are advised to put these in joint names.

GOVERNMENT OR GILT EDGED SECURITIES

Trading in government securities is referred to known as the Gilt-edged market. The government sector is a major borrower in India and government securities represent government debt to the other sectors of the economy. The government sector includes:

- The Central and State Government
- Local and municipal bodies and Semi-Government bodies, whose securities are guaranteed by either Central or State Governments. The fresh funds mobilised through the issue of government and semi-government securities have often accounted more than 80 per cent of the total amount of fresh funds mobilised through the issue of all securities on the stock market in India. The Government securities market is a significant part of it constitutes the principal segment of the debt market. If not only provides resources to the government for meeting its short term and long term needs. In india, the Government securities market is much larger than in industrial securities.

Emergence of Public Debt

The government spends more than its income by borrowing from various sources to meet the growing needs of defence, social services and planned development. The borrowing in the form of market loans in terms of rupees is the internal debt of the government and borrowing from external agencies in other currencies is its external debt. India is borrowed internal and external debt only meets its requirements of the economy. Therefore, growth for public debt the debt emergency of the government of india consists of two components, namely:

- Internal debt
- External debt

Management of Public Debt

Public debt management is concerned with following points are listed below:

- It is raising finance for the government through market loans, treasury bills and other methods.
- It is governed and managed budgetary considerations in terms of revenue and expenditure.
- Interest and repayment of debt decided by the Ministry of Finance in consultation with the RBI.

RBI Role in Debt Management

Exhibit 3.6 RBI Role in Debt Management

- To keep the cost of financing to the minimum consistent with the offer of market related interest rates on Government
- To maintains the market stable and smooth
- To lets the portfolio requirements of all investors to the extent possible.
- To maintains a minimum level of activity in the market with a view to providing liquidity to the securities in the market for the purpose of developing the market.

Principal Forms of Government Securities

There are three forms of government securities, they are:

- Stock or book debt
- Promissory notes
- Bearer bonds

Stock Certificates

Stock certificates is not a popular investment outlet for investors. Stock certificate is not transferable by mere endorsement as the execution of a transfer deed is necessary for its transfer. The stock certificate suffers from the defect of illiquidity and non-marketability. Stock certificates are the only form of government security which purchased by the Life Insurance Corporation of India and provident fund and hold it till maturity.

Promissory Notes

Promissory notes is the most popular government security. Promissory notes are highly liquid in nature especially which can be purchased by banks. The promissory note can be transferred by endorsement. Government promises to the holder of promissory notes to pay interest and amount with a specific dates. Government provides to the investors a half-yearly interest which is given only on presentation of the promissory note at the office of purchase.

Bearer Bonds

A bearer bond certifies that the bearer is entitled to a certain sum specified in rupees on the date indicated in accordance with terms of a particular loan to which the bond relates. Printed coupons for interest payable to bearer are attached to the bond. The interest is paid to the holder of the coupon and the bond is discharged on the due date of the loan to which it relates by physical presentation of the bearer. A change of ownership is effected by simple delivery of the bonds more recently, this form of loan issue was stopped by government.

Nature and Characteristics of Government Securities

Nature and characteristics of government securities are as outlined below:

Issuing Authority

Government securities are issued by the Central Government, State Government and Semi-Government authorities which include Local Government authorities like City Corporations and Municipalities, autonomous institutions like Port Trusts, Improvement Trusts, State Electricity Boards, Metropolitan Authorities, Public Sector Corporations and other Government agencies such as IDBI, IFCI, SFCs, SIDCs, NABARD, LDBs, Housing Boards, and the like.

The Central Government issues bonds, treasury bills, and special rupee securities in payment of India's subscriptions to IMF, IBRD, Asian Development Bank (ADB), International Development Association.

Government Securities and Stock Market

The stock market consists of the new issue market which is primary market for raising fresh capital, and the stock exchange which forms the secondary market for securities, each of these markets deal in two important groups of securities, namely:

- Government securities
- Industrial securities

Therefore, the stock market is associated in the minds of most people with a market for industrial securities. In fact, these constitutes a relatively small part of the stock market. Fresh funds mobilised through the issue of government and semi-government securities collected more than 80 per cent of the total amount of fresh funds mobilised through the issue of all securities on the stock market in India.

The stock market is to a large extent influenced by the government securities in India. Government securities are a unique and important financial instrument in the financial markets of any country. The government securities are controlled by the Reserve Bank of India, which maintains the statutory liquidity ratio and uses open market operations for control. Government securities constitutes the principal segment of the debt market. If not only provides resources to the government for meeting its short term and long term needs.

Government Securities and Commercial Banks

All commercial banks have to maintain their secondary resources through government securities in India. The government securities also help them to accommodation from the Reserve Bank of India whenever the need arises. Government securities are also excellent means to obtain loans. These securities are kept as collateral.

Issue Price

The government securities are normally issued in the denomination of Rs. 100 or Rs. 1,000. It has been noticed that these securities have usually been issued at a discount but not at a premium.

Government Securities and Rate of Interest

The rate of interest in government securities is relatively lower because of their being liquid and safe. The interest on government securities is payable half yearly.

Tax Exemption

Government securities is exempt from income tax subject to certain limit.

Benefits of the Government Security Holders

It is true that government security are liquid, and safe to the security holders.

Government Securities and Financial Institutions

Financial institutions have a legal constraint to invest certain proportion of their investible surplus every year in government securities. This amount is usually held by them till maturity because financial institutions find it difficult to switch from one security to another.

Government Securities and Underwriting

In the case of government securities are not underwritten, infact, brokers also do not like to deal with these types of securities. There is no need for underwriting or guaranteeing the sale of Central and State Government securities. They are issued by the Debt office of the Reserve Bank of India. This office notifies all issues and subscription which can be open for two to three days. The issues are subscribed during the year and are concentrated during the slack season. Usually, Public Debt Office tries to have a small portion of issues evenly spaced in the year according to the needs of the government budget. These securities are usually sold in 'over the counter market' and each sale is separately negotiated.

DEMATERIALISATION OF GILTED SECURITIES

In july 1998, dematerialisation of gilted securities was announced that the government securities worth Rs.5 lakh crores would be traded in a DEMAT Form from December 1998. Shares of listed PSUs will also be included in this exercise. This move is aimed at reducing paper related problems pertaining to gilts and PSU shares.

Ownership of Government Debt

The market also depends on the pattern of ownership of government debt. Pattern of ownership of government debt combined by the Central or State Government securities is published annually in their reports by the RBI.

Bonds

Bonds or debentures represent long term debt instruments. The issuer of a bond promises to pay a stipulated stream of cash flows. Bonds may be classified into the following categories:

- Government Securities
- Government of India Relief Bonds
- Government Agency Securities
- PSU Bonds
- Debentures of Private Sector Companies.

Bond is an unsecured debt of the issuer, either in the Government Sector or Corporate Sector. The Indian companies Act does not provide for bonds, but only for debentures of various categories. Basically bonds and debenture are the same and are fixed income securities.

Bond market in India is undeveloped and only banks, FIs and a few institutional investors trade in them for meeting with the legal requirements. The National Stock Exchange is expected to develop this Bond Market in India, particularly of PSUs and Government and Semi-Government bonds.

Bond Market In India

Bonds are issued by some companies, public sector financial institutions. PSUs and Semi-Government bodies in India. The secondary market in bonds in India is not well developed. Although, Companies Act, 1956 has provided for issue of debenture warrants etc., and not of bonds. since 1985, PSUs have been issuing bonds and after the start of the financial reforms and the trend of privatisation of PSUs by the government, the PSUs Public Financial Institutions etc., are all encouraged to borrow directly from the public.

Reasons For Issuing Bonds

Exhibit 3.7 Reasons for Issuing Bonds

Government borrows money due to unable to meet their expenses from current revenue. Therefore, Government still proper to go in for borrowing money for the following reasons are:

- Bonds are the cheapest source of financing. So that it reduces the cost of capital of corporation.
- EBIT brings a large change in earning per share, it result is to gain the benefit of leverage.
- Interest on bonds which is deductible from the tax and to effect of tax saving by bondholders.
- Issuing of funds bring to wide the source of funds from individual investors.
- An increase in debt does not diminish the voting power of the owners.

The Bond Indenture

The bond indenture is a legal instrument incorporating an agreement between the corporation which issue bonds, the bond holder who lends money and trustee which is either the commercial bank or trust company and represents the bondholder. In bond indenture involves three parties (a) The first party is the debtor corporation that borrows the money, promises to pay interest, and promises to repay the principal borrowed, (b) The bond holders are the second party; they lend the money. They automatically accept the indenture by acquiring their bonds, (c) The trustee is the third party with whom the bond contract is made. The trustee ensures that the corporation keeps its promises and follows the provisions contained in the indenture.

The indenture consists of

- The rate of interest or coupon rate
- Authorisation of issue
- Specimen copy of a bond
- The trustee's certificate
- The pledged property as security
- Endorsement
- Registration
- Restrictions
- Agreements
- Remedies when problems occur between trustee and bondholder
- All legal terminologies for purposes of clarity
- In case of conversion of the rights of bond holders
- In case of redemption of the rights of bond holders.

Features of Bonds

Exhibit 3.8 Features of Bonds

Maturities: Bonds are usually grouped by maturity wise classes

(a) Short term bonds
(b) Medium term bonds
(c) Long term bonds

Short term bonds usually mature within 5 years. They may be secured or unsecured.

Medium term bonds mature in 5 to 10 years. It is usually secured a real estate or equipment mortgage.

Long term bonds may run 20 years or more.

Interest: The rate of interest to be paid to the bond holder and the time of payment is recorded in the bond as well as in the indenture. The interest rate is also called the 'Coupon Rate.' Interest on bond may be made by cheque or

contd...

coupon. The bond interest is usually paid semi-annually, though annual payments are also popular. The method of payments depends upon whether the bond is a coupon or registered.

A coupon bond is one to which has been attached a number of coupons. On the other hand registered bond does not have any coupons. Each registered bond is numbered, has a payee on its face, and the debtor corporation or its agent maintains a ledger of the bond holders.

Call: Most modern corporates bonds are callable at the discretion of the issuer. This is a privilege to the issuing company to repurchase bonds at a slightly higher price above the par value.

Risk: The longer is the maturity period of bonds which is involved greater the risk and the larger percentage of changes in the price and relative to interest rate.

Pledge of Security: Bond issuing company sometimes promises to pay to the bond holders by offering some security in terms of property. The pledge of security is a promise to shareholders to writing and signed under seal and presented to the trustee by the issued company. A simple promise to pay without the agreement is not considered as a pledge of security.

Repayment of Principal: The bonds are issued in denomination of Rs. 1,000, Rs. 500 and Rs. 100 and of values as high as Rs.5, 000 to Rs. 10,000. The value of bond is called face value or par value or maturity value. The face value of bond represents the promise to repay the amount to the bond holder at the end of the specified period.

Covenants: Covenants are protective clauses in the bond indenture. They are agreements between the company and the bond holders through the trustees.

Types of Bonds

Exhibit 3.9 Types of Bonds

- Serial Bonds
- Sinking Fund Bonds
- Registered Bonds
- Debenture Bonds
- Mortgage Bonds or Secured Bonds
- Collateral Trust Bonds
- Income Bonds
- Equipment Trust Bonds
- Guarantee Bonds
- Joint Bonds
- Assumed Bonds
- Convertible Bonds and Non-Convertible Bonds
- Redeemable and Irredeemable Bonds
- Participating Bonds
- Foreign Bonds

Serial bonds: Serial bonds are not special types of bonds. Serial bonds are issued by an organisation with different maturity dates. Serial bonds is done to enable the company to repayment the bonds in instalments rather than all together. From the point view of the bond holder. He may select a short term or long term maturity. Serial bonds do not have the call feature and the company repayment the debt when it becomes payable on the maturity date.

Sinking fund bonds: Sinking fund bonds arises when the company decides to repayment its bond issue systematically by setting aside a certain amount each year for this purpose. This has the advantage of using the funds as well as repayment them without any excessive liquidity problems. The company set apart an amount annually for the retirement of bonds. Sinking fund bonds have been commonly used in industrial Finance. Therefore, it involved some risk where risk is lower.

Registered bonds: Registered bonds means the bond holders, bond numbers, name, address and type of bond are entered in the register of the issuing company. The main advantage of registering a bond are as follows:

In the case of the bond is a misplaced or lost, the bond holder does not suffer a loss unlike the unregistered bonds. Therefore, registered bonds do not offer security of principal at maturity.

Debenture bonds: Debenture bonds are issued by companies who have an excellent credit rating but do not have security in the form of assets to pledge to the bond holders. The debenture holders are creditors of the firm and receive the full rate of interest whether the company makes profit or loss.

In India, Debenture issues companies firstly obtained permission from the controller of capital issues. In the case of bearer debentures are not considered legal and permissible documents in India. In recent year, the convertible debentures have become popular because of they have lower rates of interest.

Mortgage or secured bonds: A mortgage bond is a promise by the bond issuing company to pledge in terms of real property or building. Mortgage bonds may be open end, close end, and limited open end. An open end mortgage bond permits the bonds issuing company to issue additional bonds if earnings and asset coverage make at permissible to do so.

In the case of close end mortgage bonds, the company can make only one issue of bonds and while these bonds exist, new bonds cannot be issued. If the additional bonds are issued, they get the ranking of junior bonds and the prior issue gets the first priority in receiving payments.

In the case of limited open end bonds permits the company to issue specified number of fresh bond series distributed over a number of years.

Collateral trust bonds: A collateral trust bond is issued generally when two corporation exist and are in the relationship of parent and subsidiary. Collateral trust issues are usually secured pledge in the form of shares and personal property of the company. It means that parent company can represent and control of a subsidiary corporation.

Income bonds: Income bonds are bonds. Such bonds offers interest to the bond holder only in case of firm earns a profit. If company is not earning profit sufficiently in a particular year, interest on bonds is cumulated for a future period when the company can sufficiently earn and make a profit. Income bonds are not offered for sale as new financing but are often issued in reorganisation or recapitalisation to replace other securities.

Equipment trust bonds: Equipment trust bonds is issued on the USA, a typical example of equipment trust bonds is issue of bonds with equipment like machinery as security. The property papers are submitted to trustees. These bonds are retired serially. The usual method of using these bonds was to issue 20% equity and 80% bonds. The equity issue is like a reserve to protect the lender in cases where the value of the assets falls in the market. The trustee also has the right to sell the equipment and pay the bondholders in case of default.

Guaranteed bonds: Bonds may be guaranteed by the issuing company and they are guarantied by another company. Several times, a company takes asset through a lease, the leasing company guarantees the bonds of the bond issuing company regarding interest and principal amount due on the bonds.

Joint Bonds: Joint bonds are loan certificates that are jointly secured by two or more companies. These bonds are issued when two or more companies are in need of finance and decide to raise funds together through bonds. The company raises funds at reduced cost. Since funds are raised jointly, dual operations of advertising and the formalities of capital issues control are avoided.

Assumed bonds: Assumed bonds are issues in respect of a company that has been acquired by another by way of merger or as a result of the reorganisation. In taking over the property of the original issuer the debts of the issuer are assumed by the successor company.

Convertible bonds and non-convertible bonds: Convertible bonds holder can at his option to convert the bond into a predetermined number of shares of common stock at predetermined price.

In the case of non-convertible bonds holder cannot at his option to convert the bond into a predetermined number of shares of common stock at predetermined price.

Redeemable and irredeemable bonds: A redeemable debenture is bond which has been issued for a certain period after expiry of which its holder will be repaid the amount with or without premium. A bond without the aforesaid redemption period is termed as an irredeemable debenture. Irredeemable bonds may be repaid either in the event of the liquidation of the company.

Participating bonds: Companies are those poor credit positions to be issued participating bonds. These bonds have a guaranteed rate of interest but may also participate in earnings upto additional specified percentage.

Foreign bonds: Bonds raised in india by Foreign Companies but for Indian investor will be called a 'Foreign Bond'.

POST OFFICE SAVINGS DEPOSITS

Post Office Schemes are similar to fixed deposits of commercial banks. They have a saving account, a recurring account, a ten-year cumulative time deposit account which are also recurring in nature. The post office schemes are the saving media. The major post office schemes enjoy tax concessions in terms of exemption of investment contribution from tax or interest income from tax or both up to certain limits.

Post Office Time Deposits (POTDs)

Exhibit 3.10 Features of Post Office Time Deposits

- Deposits can be made in multiples of Rs. 50 without any limit.
- The interest rates POTDs are, in general, slightly higher than those on bank deposits.
- The interest is calculated half yearly and paid annually.
- No withdrawal is permitted upto six months.
- After six months, withdrawals are permitted on withdrawals made between six months and one year, no interest is payable. On withdrawals after one year, but before the term of deposit interest is paid for the deposit has been held, subject to a penal deduction of 2 per cent.
- A POTDs account can be pledged.
- The interest POTDs is exempt within certain limits under Section 80L of the Income Tax Act.

Monthly Income Scheme of the Post Office (MISPO)

Exhibit 3.11 Features of Monthly Income Scheme of the Post Office

MISPO is the popular scheme of the post office. It is mean to provide regular monthly income to the depositors. The salient features of this scheme are as follows:

- The term of the scheme is 6 years.
- The minimum amount of investment is Rs. 1,000. The maximum investment can be Rs. 3,00,000 in a single account or Rs. 6,00,000 in a joint account.
- The interest rate is 9.0 per cent payable monthly. A bonus of 10 per cent is payable on the maturity.
- Interest income is tax exempt within certain limits as per Section 80L of the Income Tax Act.
- There is no tax deduction at source.
- There is a facility of premature withdrawal after one year, with 5% deduction before 3 years.

Kisan Vikas Patra (KVP)

Exhibit 3.12 Features of Kisan Vikas Patra

The Kisan Vikas Patra has the following features:

- The minimum amount of investment is Rs.1,000. There is no maximum limit.
- The investment doubles in 7 years and 8 months. Hence, the compound interest rate works out to 9.46 per cent.
- There is no tax deduction at source.
- KVPs can be pledged as a collateral security for raising loans.
- There is a withdrawal facility after $2\frac{1}{2}$ years.

National Savings Certificate

Exhibit 3.13 Features of National Savings Certificate

National Savings Certificate are issued at Post Offices. An important features of National Savings Certificate. They are:

- It comes in denominations of Rs.100, Rs.500, Rs. 1,000, Rs. 5,000 and Rs.10,000.
- It has a term of 6 years. Over this period Rs. 100 becomes Rs.169.59. Hence the compound rate of return works out to 9.20 per cent.
- The investment in NSC is eligible for 20 per cent tax exemption under Section 88 upto a certain limit.
- The interest accruing every year qualifies for exemption u/s 80L.
- There is no tax deduction at source.
- It can be pledged as a collateral for raising loans.

National Savings Scheme

Exhibit 3.14 Features of National Savings Scheme

An important features are:

- Only individual and HUFs are eligible to participate in this scheme. An NSS account can be opened at designated post offices.
- An amount of up to Rs. 40,000 per year can be deposited in an NSS account. The deposit qualifies for tax rebate under Section 88 of the Income Tax Act.
- The NSS account earns a compound interest rate of 9.0 per cent per annum. This is accumulated in the account itself and is not taxed at the time of accrual.
- The balance is an NSS account is exempt from wealth tax.
- After an initial lock in period of three years, one withdrawal is permitted annually. The amount that can be withdrawn is limited to the balance at the end of the fourth preceding year.
- The amount that is withdrawn during a year is taxable.
- If a subscriber to an NSS account dies, his/her successor is not liable to be taxed on the withdrawal.
- While the NSS account has no defined maturity period, it can be closed at the option of the subscriber after the expiry of three years from the end of the year in which the last deposit made.

Employees Provident Fund Schemes

Exhibit 3.15 Features of Employees Provident Fund Schemes

Employees Provident Fund schemes is a major vehicles of savings for salaried employees. The major features of employees provident fund schemes as outlined below:

- Each employee has a separate provident fund account in which both the employer and the employee are required to contribute a certain minimum amount a monthly basis.
- If the employee can choose to contribute additional amounts, subject to certain restrictions.
- While the contribution made by the employer is fully exempt (from the point of view of the employee), the contribution made by the employee qualify for tax rebate under Section 88 of the Income Tax Act.
- Provident fund contributions earn a compound interest rate of 9.5 per cent per annum this is totally exempt from taxes. The interest, however, is accumulated in the provident fund and not paid annually to the employee.
- The balance in the provident fund account is fully exempt from wealth tax. Further, it is not subject to attachment under any order or decree of a court.
- Within a certain limit, the employee is eligible to take a loan against the provident fund balance pertaining to his contributions only.

QUESTIONS FOR DISCUSSIONS

1. What do you mean by investment opportunities?
2. Name the different type of non-marketable financial assets.
3. Explain the fixed income securities.
4. What do you mean by equity shares?
5. What are the characteristics of equity shares?
6. Describe the advantages of equity shares.
7. What are rights of equity shareholders?
8. Explain the classification of equity shares.
9. What is preference shares? What are characteristics of the preference shares?
10. Briefly explain the different types of preference shares.
11. What is Debentures? Briefly explain the classification of debenture?
12. What is fixed deposit companies? What are the terms and condition of acceptance of fixed deposit?
13. What are the complaints regarding the fixed deposit companies?
14. What is Government (Gilt edge) Security?
15. Briefly explain the RBI role in Debt Management.
16. What are the principal forms of Government securities?
17. Briefly describe the nature and characteristic of Government securities.
18. What is demateralisation of gilt edge securities?
19. What is bonds? What are the reasons for issuing bonds?
20. What is importance of Bond Indenture?
21. Briefly explain the features of bonds.
22. Briefly describe the different types of bonds.
23. What is post office savings deposits?
24. What are the features of post office time deposits?
25. Briefly explain the features of monthly income scheme of the post office.
26. Briefly describe the features of KVP.
27. Briefly explain the National Saving Certificate features.
28. Briefly explain the features of Employee Provident Scheme.

■■■

CHAPTER 4

INVESTMENT OPPORTUNITIES-II

Learning Objectives

- What are investment opportunities for individual and small investor.
- Explain which investment opportunities is benefited to small investors, Government employees, businessmen, professional and common people
- Discuss the different features of different investment opportunities.

INTRODUCTION

In this chapter, we shall outlook for:

- Provident Fund
- Unit Trust of India
- Money Market Instrument
- Bank Deposits
- Precious Objects
- LIC
- Real Estate
- Chit Funds
- Mutual Funds

The previous chapter has discussed about company shares, debentures, fixed deposit of companies, Government or Gilt edged securities, bonds, post office savings deposits and employee provident fund schemes.

PROVIDENT FUND

Provident fund promotes savings and makes a provision for the old age of an employee. Under the scheme, a specific amount is deducted from the salary of an employee every month which is credited to his account in the provident fund. The employer is also obliged to contribute a stipulated amount every month to the credit of employee's account in the provident fund. The total amount consists of employee's and employer's contributions, is invested in Government Securities or deposited in a bank. The interest of such investment is also credited to the employee's account. The contribution made by an employer and the employee and interest on such contributions get multiplied over years. The accumulated balance is paid to an employee on his retirement or on his leaving the service. In the event of death, the accumulated balance is paid to the legal heirs of a deceased employee.

Types/Kinds of Provident Fund

There are mainly four kinds/types of Provident Fund.

- Statutory Provident Fund
- Recognised Provident Fund
- Unrecognised Provident Fund
- Public Provident Fund

Statutory Provident Fund

Statutory provident fund is set up under the Provident Fund Act, 1925. Such fund is maintained in Government Offices, Reserve Bank of India, State Bank of India, Railways, Statutory Corporation, Universities and Colleges.

Recognised Provident Fund

It is a provident fund which has been and continues to be recognised by the commissioner in accordance with the rules contained in Part A of the Fourth Schedule to the Income Tax Act. It also includes a fund established under the Employee's Provident Act, 1952. Such a fund is maintained in bank's Insurance Companies, factories and business houses in private sector.

Unrecognised Provident Fund

A fund which is not recognised by the Commissioner of the Income Tax Department, is known as "unrecognised fund". It can be maintained by any institution in private sector.

Public Provident Fund

In the case of Public Provident Fund employer contribution does not arise any amount. Public provident fund is a one type fund which provide for non-salaried people to mobilise personal savings. Any person from the public whether salaried or self employed, can open a public provident fund account to any branch of the State Bank of India.

Features of Public Provident Fund (PPF)

Exhibit 4.1 Features of Public Privident Fund

- Any person from the public whether salaried or self employed can participate in this scheme. A PPF account may be opened at any branch of State Bank of India or its subsidiaries.
- The subscriber to a PPF account is required to make minimum deposit of Rs.100 and maximum is Rs. 70,000 per year.
- PPF deposits earn a cumulative interest rate of 9 per cent per annum, which is totally exempt from tax.
- PPF account has a maturity period of 15 years.
- PPF cannot be transferable but it has provided nomination facility to the subscriber.
- The balance in a PPF account is fully exempt from wealth tax.
- All subscriptions to PPF are completely Tax free.
- Withdrawal per financial year can be made any time after 5 years from the end the year in which subscription is made.
- Subscriber withdrawal is limited to 50% of the balance at the end of the Fourth Year.

UNIT TRUST OF INDIA

Unit Trust of India is a public sector financial institution. The UTI was created with the aim of mobilising saving of the small man (small investors) and reinvesting these funds into different investment outlets. Unit Trust of India is managed by a competent Board of Trustees. UTI Chairman is appointed by the Central Government. UTI consists of an Executive Trustee and Four other members who looks after for savings of the investors. These members are appointed by the Industrial Development Bank of India, Reserve Bank of India, Life Insurance Corporation of India and sometimes by commercial banks. UTI is offering an attractive return and growth to the investors while minimising the risk elements for individual investors.

Unit Trust of India began its operations with Five crores of rupees that jointly subscribed by industrial Development Bank of India, Life Insurance Corporation of India, State Bank of India, Commercial Banks and other financial institutions. Rs. Five Crore was given to UTI as the initial amount of the capital. The Unit capital varies from year to year and depends on the subscription of the investors.

Functions of Unit Trust of India

Exhibit 4.2 Functions of Unit Trust of India

An important functions of Unit Trust of India

- It's offering an attractive return and growth to be individual investors and small savers
- It's minimising the risk for small investors
- It's directing lending of funds
- It is involved bill rediscounting
- Leasing
- Financing of Housing projects
- Hire purchasing finance
- It has set up subsidiaries for many financial services and banking.

Objectives of Investing in Units

Exhibit 4.3 Objectives of Unit Trust of India

- Unit Trust of India assures to investor a safe return of the investment
- Unit Trust of India also provided tax benefits upto certain limits
- Liquidity of the Unit Trust of India units
- It gives up date information about unit investment to small investors
- Its mobilising savings from individual and small investors and redeployment in productive projects

Unit Trust of India Schemes

Exhibit 4.4 Unit Trust of India Schemes

- Unit Scheme 1964
- Reinvestment Plan 1966
- Children's Gift Plan 1970
- Unit Linked Insurance Plan 1971
- Unit Scheme for Charitable and Religious Trust and Registered Societies 1981
- Capital Gains Unit Scheme 1983
- Income Unit Scheme 1985

contd...

- Children College and Carrier Fund Unit Plan
- Grahalakshmi Unit Plan 1994
- Senior Citizen Plan
- Scheme for Charitable and Religious Trusts and Societies
- Institutional Investors Special Fund Unit Schemes 1993
- Bhopal Gas Victims mainly Income Plan 1992
- Monthly Income Unit Scheme
- Seven Year Monthly Income Scheme
- Income Unit Scheme
- Deferred Income Unit Scheme
- Unit Growth Scheme 2000
- Mutual Fund Unit Scheme 1986 Master Share
- Master Equity Plan 1991
- Capital Growth Unit Scheme 1991
- Capital Growth Unit Scheme 1992

MONEY MARKET INSTRUMENT

Money market is a market for short term loans or financial assets. It is market for the lending and borrowing of short term funds. It does not actually deal in cash or money. Therefore, it actually deals with money market instrument like as:

- Treasury bills
- Certificates of Deposits (CD)
- Commercial paper
- Repos

Features of a Money Market

Exhibit 4.5 Features of a Money Maket

- It is a market purely for short term funds or financial assets called near money.
- It deals with debt instrument which have a maturity of less than one year at the time of issue are called money market instruments.
- Money market instruments are highly liquid and have negligible risk.
- The money market is dominated by the government, financial institutions, banks and corporates.
- Money market transactions have to be conducted without help of the brokers.
- It consists of sub-markets, each speculising in a particular type of financing. For example, call money market, acceptance market, bill market and so on.

Objectives of Money Market

Exhibit 4.6 Objectives of Money Market

An important objectives of money market outlooks for:

- It provides a parking place to employ short term surplus funds
- It provides room for overcoming short term deficits
- It enable to the Central Bank to influence and regulate liquidity in the economy through its intervention in the market
- It provides a reasonable access to users of short term funds to meet their requirement quickly, adequately and at reasonable costs.

TREASURY BILLS

Treasury bills are the most important money market instrument. They represent short term borrowings of the government. Treasury bill market refers to the market where treasury bills are bought and sold. Treasury bills are very popular and enjoy a higher degree of liquidity since they are issued by government. Treasury bills are issued only by the RBI on behalf of the government. Treasury bills are issued for meeting temporary government deficits. The treasury bill rate or the rate of discount is fixed by the RBI from time to time. It is short term maturity and high degree of liquidity and security.

Though the yield on Treasury bills is somewhat how, yet they have an appeal for the following reasons:

- These can be transacted readily and there is a very active in secondary market
- Treasury bills have nil credit risk and without risk.

Certificates of Deposits

Certificate of Deposits (CDs) refers to short term deposits which are transferable from one party to another. Certificate of Deposits are short term deposit instruments issued by banks and financial institutions to raise sums of money.

Features of Certificate of Deposit

Exhibit 4.7 Features of Certificate of Deposit

An important features of certificate of deposit:
- Document of title to time deposit
- Unsecured negotiable pronotes
- Freely transferable by endorsement and delivery
- Issued at discount to face value
- Repayable on a fixed date without grace days
- Subject to stamp duty like the usance promissory notes.

Advantages of Certificate Deposits

Exhibit 4.8 Advantages of Certificate Deposits

- Certificate of deposits are the most convenient instruments to depositors as they enable their short term surpluses to earn higher return
- A CDs are generally offered a higher rate of interest than Treasury bills or term deposits
- CDs are generally offered maximum liquidity
- CDs are transferable by endorsement and delivery
- CDs holders can resell his certificate to another
- CDs are generally risk free
- Financial institutions are normally willing to tailor the denominations and maturities to suit the needs of the investors.

COMMERCIAL PAPER

A commercial paper is an unsecured promissory note issued with a fixed maturity by a company approved by RBI, negotiable by endorsement and delivery, issued in bearer form and issued at discount on the face value as may be determined by the issuing company.

Features of Commercial Papers

Exhibit 4.9 Features of Commercial Papers

- Commercial paper is a short term money market instruments.
- It is comprising usance promissory note with a fixed maturity.
- Commercial paper is issued at a discount to face value base and it can also be issued in interest bearing form.
- Commercial paper can be issued directly by a company to investors or through banks/merchant bankers.
- A commercial paper usually has a maturity period of 90 to 180 days.

Advantages of Commercial Paper

Simplicity

Simplicity is an obvious advantages of commercial paper. It involves hardly any documentation between the issuer and investor.

Flexibility

Issuer can issue commercial paper with the maturities tailored to match the cash flow of the company.

Diversification

A well rated company can diversify its source of finance from banks to short term money markets at somewhat cheaper cost.

Easy to Raise Long Term Capital

The companies which are able to raise funds through commercial paper become better known in the financial world and are thereby placed in a more favourable position for raising such long term capital as they may, from time to time, require. Thus there is an in built incentive for companies to remain financially strong.

High Returns

The commercial paper provides higher returns to investors than they get from the banking system.

Movement of Funds

Commercial paper facilitates securitisation of loans resulting in creation of a secondary market for the paper and efficient movement of funds are providing cash surplus to cash deficit entities.

REPOS

The term REPO stand for Repurchase Agreement or Ready Forward. A Repo involves a simultaneous "Sale and Repurchase" agreement. Under Repo transaction, the borrower parts with securities to the lender with an agreement to repurchase them at the end of the fixed period at a specified price. At the end of the period, the borrower will repurchase the securities at the predetermined prices. The difference between price and the original price is the cost for the borrower. This cost of borrowing is called "Repo Rate" which is little cheaper than pure borrowing.

Repos are a very convenient instrument for short term investment. They are safe and earn a pre-determined return.

BANK DEPOSITS

Indian banks accept two main types of deposits. They are:

- Demand Deposits
- Term Deposits

Demand Deposits

Demand deposits can be sub-divided into two categories:

- Current Account
- Savings Account

Current deposits are checkable accounts and there are no restrictions on the amount or the number of withdrawals from these accounts. It is possible to obtain or secured overdraft on current account. At present, banks generally do not pay interest on current deposits.

Saving deposits earn interest. The rate of interest is paid at 3.5%, which is the lowest among the various categories of investments.

Although cheques can be drawn on savings accounts, the number of withdrawals and the maximum amount that might, at any time be withdrawn from an account without previous notice are restricted.

Call deposits is the third sub-category of demand deposits. They are accepted from fellow bankers and are repayable on demand. These deposits carry an interest charge.

Time Deposits

Time deposits are also known as fixed deposits or term deposits and they are a genuine saving medium. They have different maturity periods on which depends the rate of interest.

PRECIOUS OBJECTS

Precious objects are items which are generally small in size but highly valuable in monetary terms. The important precious objects are:

- Gold and Silver
- Precious Stones
- Art Objects
- Antiques

Gold and Silver

Gold and silver are an important precious objects. Gold and silver appeal to almost all types of investors for the reasons as outlined below:

- They have been good hedges against inflation
- They are generally highly liquid with very low trading commissions
- Gold and silver aesthetically attractive
- According to Jack Francis Gold and silver possess a high degree of moneyness.

Disadvantages of Gold and Silver

Exhibit 4.10 Disadvantages of Gold and Silver

The following disadvantages of gold and silver

- Gold and silver do not provide regular current income
- There is no tax benefits associated with them
- Many times, they may be cheated
- Gold and Silver have not kept up with inflation in recent times, due to softening of their prices

Precious Stones

Precious stones are as below:

- Diamonds
- Rubies
- Emeralds
- Sapphires
- Pearls

These have appealed to investors from times immemorial because of their aesthetic appeal and rarity. Especially, diamond have attracted to investors because of their high per carat value. The quality of diamond is basically judged in terms of carat, colour, cut and clarity. The investor must be cautious to buy diamonds because each jeweler decides the value of the diamond according to his own judgement.

Precious Stones can be very illiquid. It may not be easy to sell them quickly. It is an extremely risky form of investment. It requires huge investments. Precious stones do not earn a regular return during the period are held by investors.

Art Objectives

Art objectives possess aesthetic appeal because their production requires in terms of salad, taste, creativity, talent and imagination may be referred to as art objects. Art objects are as below:

- Paintings
- Sculptures
- Etchings

Its aesthetic appeal, rarity, reputation of the creator, physical condition and fashion are decided the value of art objects.

Antiques

Antiques may be in the form of paintings, coin, stamps, a manuscript, a sculpture, flower vases, watches, cars or any other object. In the case demand is more and supply is very rare that its impact is increase the value of the antiques. It is very risky for long holding period investment.

LIFE INSURANCE CORPORATION

There has been Life Insurance business in India since 1818. Till 1956, the insurance business was mixed and decentralised. There were a large number of companies (245 on the eve of nationalisation) of different ages, sizes, and patterns of organisations which conducted only life insurance business, and there were some companies whose main business was general insurance but which did life insurance also.

In 1956, The Life Insurance business of all companies as mentioned was nationalised and a single monolithic organisation, The Life Insurance Corporation of India was set up. Today, Life Insurance is almost entirely in the hands of the LIC.

Objectives of the LIC

Exhibit 4.11 Objectives of the LIC

The objectives of the LIC are:

- To spread life insurance and provides life insurance protection to the mass at reasonable cost.
- To mobilise people's savings through insurance linked saving schemes.
- To invest the funds to serve the best interests of both the policy holders and nation.
- To conduct business with maximum economy, always remembering that the money belongs to the policy holders.
- To act as trustees of the policy holders and protect their individual and collective interests.
- To innovate and adapt to meet the changing life insurance needs of the community.
- To involve all the people working in the corporation to ensure efficient and courteous service to the insured public.
- To promote amongst all agents and employees of the corporation a sense of pride and job satisfaction through dedicated service to achieve the corporate objective.

Diversification of LIC

The LIC has diversified its activities as below:

- LIC Housing Finance Ltd.
- LIC Mutual Fund
- Jeevan Bima Sahayog Asset Management Company
- LIC (International)

LIC as a Investment

Exhibit 4.12 LIC as a Investment

Life Insurance is called as investment because of a number of reasons given below:

- It provides protection against risk of early death.
- It can be used as a collateral for taking loans from banks.
- Life of key men in an association can be protected.
- It provides tax advantages.
- It is a measure of protection at the time of death because it gives provision for estate duty.
- It is a sum of money received at the end of a particular number of years.

Types of Policies

The common types of Life Insurance Policy are:

- Whole Life Policy
- Endowment Policy
- Term Policy
- Money Back Plan Policy
- Immediate Annuity Policy
- Deferred Annuity Policy

Whole Life Policy

Whole life policy provides a benefit on the death of the policy holder whenever that might happen. The insurer do not gets benefit but his family receive the amount after his death.

Advantages of the Whole Life Policy

Exhibit 4.13 Advantages of the Whole Life Policy

- It provides long term financial protection to the dependent
- Insurer does not enjoy the life policy as an investment himself because the return will only after his death. It is only benefit for his dependent
- It is useful for a person who would like to profit for payment of estate duty on his property if he/she dies
- The lowest rate of premium is compared to other policies. In the case a person insures himself at an early age, he/she can obtain a large amount of insurance for small premium.

The whole life policy may be issued in the following way:

- Non-participating policy
- Participating policy

Non-participating policies principally offers a guaranteed sum assured on death. Non-participating policy generally, the initial guaranteed sum assured may be increased by in terms of cash or bonus refund may be given. Where the initial guaranteed sum assured is increased by bonuses, the sum assured together with the accrued bonuses becomes payable on the death of the policyholder.

Endowment Policy

The endowment insurance Policy is the best form of investment to an investor who aims to take life policy as a form of investment. Major benefits to policy holders:

- Saving his income
- Protection to life
- Receiving tax benefits

Under this plan, the insurance company promises to pay a stated amount of money to the beneficiary, in the case insured dies during the period of life policy. He/she got policy amount. Endowment policies may be issued in different forms. These are:

- Non-participating endowment policy
- Participating endowment policy

Term Policy

Term policy is a pure protection policy that provides a benefit on the death of an individual within a specified term. Term insurance policy is a contract for payment of amount insured only if the insured dies during the term of the policy or specified period stated within the contract. If the insured does not die during the specified period, the contract expires and is treated as cancelled. This policy can be used and meet two such specific needs, namely:

- It can be used to repay the balance outstanding under a loan in the event of death of the policy holder.
- It can be used to provide an income of the family of the deceased policy holder from the time of death up to the end of the policy term.

Money Back Plan Policy

Money Back Plan Policy is a popular savings cum protection policy because it provides lumpsum at periodic intervals. This policy is usually sweetened by providing a guaranteed addition to the initial sum assured every year.

Immediate Annuity Policy

Immediate Annuity Policy meets the policyholder's need for regular income, for example, after his retirement. The policy can also be structured to provide an income for a limited period. For example, to pay the school fees of the policyholder's children.

Deferred Annuity Policy

The usual structure of Deferred Annuity Policy is that the policyholder pays regular premiums for a period up to the specified "Vesting date". These premiums buy amounts of regular income payable to the policyholder from the vesting date. A single premium at the start of the policy is a possible alternative to regular premiums.

A deferred annuity enables the policyholder to build up a pension that becomes payable on his or her retirement from gainful employment. At the vesting date of the annuity, the alternative a lumpsum may be offered in lieu of part or all of the pension, thereby meeting any need for a cash sum at that point, for example to pay off a housing loan.

REAL ESTATE

Real estate differs from security investments in two ways:

- It involves ownership of a tangible asset - real property rather than a financial claim.
- Managerial decisions about real estate greatly affect the returns earned from investment in it. Real estate means "Buying right" or "Selling right". It also means managing the property right.

Real Estate investments further classified into two broad categories. They are:

- Income Properties
- Speculative Properties

Income Properties

Income properties are the residential and commercial properties that are leased out and expected to provide returns primarily from period of rental income.

Residential Properties

Residential properties include single family properties (houses, co-operatives).

Commercial Properties

Commercial properties include:

- Office buildings
- Shopping centres
- Warehouses
- Factories

Speculative Properties

Speculative properties include raw land and investment properties that are expected to provide returns primarily from appreciation in value due to location, scarcity, etc.

Types of Real Estate

A residential house is the most important asset for individual investors. The investors are likely to be interested in the following types of real estate. They are:

- Residential House
- Commercial Property
- Agriculture Land
- Suburban Land
- Time Share in a Holiday Resort

Residential House

A residential house represents an attractive investment due to the following reasons. They are:

- The total return in terms of rental savings plus capital appreciation.
- Loans are available from various source for buyings/ constructing a residential property.
- In the case of wealth tax purposes, the value of a residential property is calculated at its historical cost and not at its present market price.
- Interest on loans taken for buying/constructing a residential house which is tax deductible within certain limits.
- Ownership of a residential property provides psychological satisfaction for individual investors.

Commercial Property

The investors are interesting to invest in commercial property. Commercial property may take of constructing a commercial complex or buying office or shop space in a commercial complex.

The investors are interesting to invest in commercial property due to mainly in the form of regular rental income which can be revised upward periodically. In additionally, the commercial property may enjoy some capital appreciation over a period of time. The main disadvantages is that requires a large outlay and may require time and effort in managing it.

Agricultural Land

Agriculture land is an attractive investment for investors due to the following reasons:

- Agricultural income is exempt from tax.
- Agricultural land is exempt from wealth tax.
- Different types of loans are available for agriculture operations at a concessional rate.
- Agricultural land value is the appreciation.

Some times agriculture land is not attractive investment due to the following reasons:

- In many states, land ceiling are quite restrictive.
- Many state laws that confers ownership to the cultivating tenant.
- Agricultural operation is an uneconomical or unprofitable activity.

Suburban Land

Suburban land means land within city limits. This land is very costly. Therefore, you can buy residential land in private layouts in suburban areas at highly prices. Suburban land investment offers for capital appreciation. In additionally, it gives you an opportunity to move to quieter location that may not be very distance from the city as the city expands.

MUTUAL FUNDS

Presently, mutual funds have become a not favourable of millions of people all over the world. The driving force of mutual fund is that the 'safety of the principal' guaranteed, in additionally advantage of capital appreciation together with the income earned in the form of interest or dividend. Generally people are preferred mutual funds to bank deposits, life insurance and even bonus because with a little money, they can get into the investment game. Therefore, mutual fund act as a gateway to enter into big companies hitherto inaccessible to an ordinary investor with his small investment.

What is a Mutual Fund?

In general meaning, a mutual fund mobilising the savings from small investors, invest them in Government and other corporate securities and earn income through interest and dividends, besides capital gains. It works on the general principal of "small drops of water make a big ocean". For example, if one has invest Rs. 1,000, it may not fetch very much on its own. Therefore, when it is pooled with Rs. 1,000 each from a lot of other people, then, one could create a 'big fund' large enough to invest in a wide varieties of shares and debentures on a commanding scale and thus, to enjoy the economies of large scale operations. However, a mutual fund is nothing but a form of mobilising investment from the small investors who transfer their saving into a professionally qualified organisation to manage it.

Mutual fund has emerged as a popular vehicle of creation of wealth due to high return, lower cost and diversified risk.

Definition of Mutual Funds

According to the Securities and Exchange Board of India (Mutual Funds) Regulations, 1993 defines the term 'Mutual Fund' as "a fund established in the form of a trust by a sponsor, to raise monies by the trustees through the sale of units to the public, under one or more schemes, for investing in securities in accordance with these regulations".

According to the Kaman, J.O. has defines an open end investment company as "an organisation formed for the investment of funds obtained from individuals and institutional investors who in exchange for the funds receive shares which can be redeemed at any time at their underlying asset values."

According to Weston J. Fred and Brigham, Eugene, F., Unit Trusts are "Corporation which accept dollars from savers and then use these dollars to buy stocks, long term bonds, short term debt instruments issued by business or government units: these corporations pool funds and reduce risk by diversification."

All these definitions reveals that the mutual funds are corporations which pool funds by selling their own shares and reduce risk by diversification.

Origin of the Fund/Concept of the Mutual Fund

The origin of the mutual fund dates back to the very dawn of commercial history. It is said that Egyptians and Phoenicians sold their shares in vessels and caravans with a view to spread the risk attached with these risky ventures. However, the real credit of introducing the modern concept of mutual fund goes to the Foreign and Colonial Government Trust of London established in 1868. Thereafter, a large number of close ended mutual funds were formed in the USA in 1930s followed by many countries in Europe, the Far East and Latin America. In most of countries, both open end and close ended types were popular. In India, it gained momentum only in 1980, though it began in the year 1964 with Unit Trust of India launching its first fund, under the Unit Scheme 1964.

Mutual Fund Schemes in India

Till 1986 the Unit Trust of India was the only mutual fund in India. From there on Public Sector Banks and Insurance Companies were allowed to set up their subsidiaries to undertake mutual fund business. An important mutual fund schemes are:

- State Bank of India, Canara Bank, LIC, GIC and few public sector banks funds
- From 1992 onwards the mutual fund industry was opened to the private sectors as examples are: Alliance Capital Mutual Fund, Birla Mutual Fund, DSP Merrill Lynch Mutual fund, HDFC Mutual Fund, IDBI-Principal Mutual Fund, JM Mutual Fund, Kotak Mahindra Mutual Fund, Morgan Stanley Mutual

Fund, Pioneer ITI Mutual Fund, Prudential ICICI Mutual Fund, Reliance Mutual Fund, Standard Chartered Mutual Fund, Tata Mutual Fund, Templetion India Mutual Fund and Zurich India Mutual Fund.

Type of Mutual Funds/Classification of Mutual Fund

Mutual Funds Schemes can broadly classified as below:

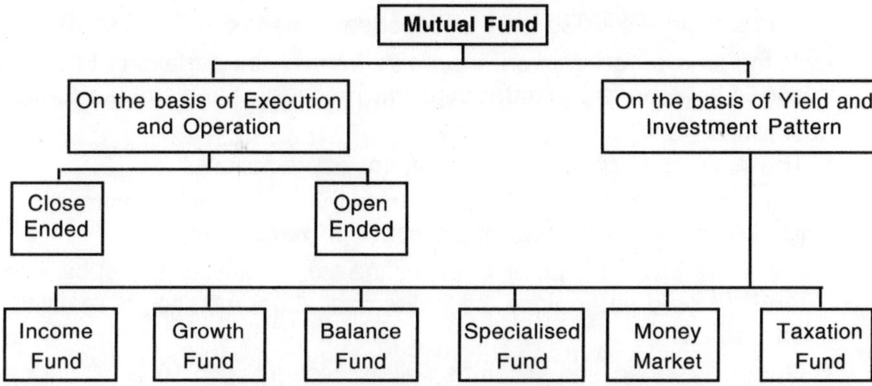

Fig. 4.1 Classification of Mutual Fund

Figure 4.1 Indicates the classification of mutual fund as below:

- On the basis of Execution and Operation
- On the basis of Yield and Investment pattern

On the Basis of Execution and Operation

Mutual fund further classified on the basis of execution and operation. They are

- Close Ended Funds
- Open Ended Funds

Close ended funds

Under this scheme, the subscription (collection of fund) is open only for limited period usually it is one month to three months. In other sense, under this scheme, the collection of the fund and the number of units are determined in advance. Once the subscription reaches the predetermined level, the entry of investors is closed. A close end scheme does not allow investors to withdraw funds as and when they like. The close end schemes are listed on the secondary market.

Features of Close Ended Funds

Exhibit 4.14 Features of Close Ended Funds

- The subscription opens for investors only for limited period.
- Once subscription period is over or target is reached, the door is closed for the investors.
- It does not allow investors to withdraw their funds as and when they like.
- This scheme is listed on the secondary market.
- At the time of redemption, the entire investment pertaining to a close ended scheme is liquidated and the proceeds are distributed among the subscribers.
- The main goal of this fund is capital appreciation.
- From the market point of view the full value of the investment may not be realised because of an adverse market impact.
- From the investors point of view, the tax liability of the subscribers tends to be greater since the entire capital appreciation is realised in one go itself.
- Generally, close end schemes sell at discount upto 10 to 30 per cent below their net asset value.

Open ended eunds

Open Ended Funds is just opposite of close end funds under this scheme, it accepts fund from investors by offering its units o· shares on a continuing basis. This scheme permits investor to withdraw funds on a continuing basis under a repurchase arrangement. In this scheme, there is no maturity periods to units. Open end funds are not listed in stock exchange. The investors are free to buy and sell them any number of units at any point of time.

Features of the Open Ended Funds

Exhibit 4.15 Features of Open Ended Funds

- Under this scheme, there is free entry and exist of investors. There is no time limit, the investor can join in and come out from the fund as and when he desires.
- These funds are not listed in secondary market.
- The main objective of this fund is income generation. Investors are got expected return from their return in terms of dividend and bonus.
- Net Asset value of the fund is fluctuate from time to time.
- The fund manager can plan and managements in better.

Difference between Close End and Open End Funds

Exhibit 4.16 Difference between Close End and Open End Funds

Close End Fund	*Open End Fund*
• The corpus is open only for limited period.	• The corpus is open on continuous basis.
• It does not allow investors to withdraw funds as and when they like.	• It can allow investors to withdraw funds whenever require.
• This scheme maturity period is fixed.	• In this, no maturity is fixed.
• This fund schemes are listed on the secondary market.	• This fund schemes are not listed on the secondary market.

On the basis of Yield and Investment Pattern

Mutual fund further classified on the basis of yield and investment pattern. they are:

- Income Fund
- Growth Fund
- Balance Fund
- Specialised Fund
- Money Market
- Taxation Fund

Income funds

Income funds main aims at generating and distributing regular income to the subscribers (Investors) on a periodical basis. It concentrates more on distribution of regular income in terms dividend. Income funds is suitable to the old and retired people who may not have any regular income.

Growth funds

Growth funds concentrates mainly on long run gains. It means capital appreciation. They do not offer regular income and they aim at capital appreciation in the long run. Hence, they have been explained as "Nest Eggs" investments.

Balanced funds

Balance funds also known as "Income-cum-Growth" Fund. It is a combination of both income and growth funds. It aims at distributing regular income as well as capital appreciation. This is achieved by balancing the investments between the high growth equity shares and also the fixed income earning securities.

Specialised funds

A large number of specialised funds are in existence abroad. They offer special schemes so as to meet the specific needs of specific categories of people like pensioners, widows etc. For instance, Japan Fund, South Korea Fund etc.

Money Market mutual funds

Money market mutual funds are basically open ended mutual funds are as such they have all the features of the open ended fund. But they investment in highly liquid and safe securities like commercial paper, banker's acceptance, certificates of deposits, Treasury bills etc.

Taxation funds

A taxation fund is basically a growth oriented fund. But, it offers tax rebates to the investors either in the domestic or foreign capital market. It suitable to salaried people who want to enjoy tax rebates particularly during the month of February and March.

Index funds

Index fund refers to those funds where the portfolios are designed in such a way that they reflect the composition of some broad based market index. This is done by holding securities in the same proportion as they index itself.

Importance of Mutual Funds

Exhibit 4.17 Importance of Mutual Funds

- Channelising and mobilising savings for investment.
- It is offering wide folio investment in different schemes.
- Mutual funds are providing better yields to investors.
- Mutual fund companies are rendering expertised investment service at low cost.
- Mutual fund companies are mobilising corpus from individual investors, therefore, they are providing research service.
- Mutual funds are widely offering tax benefits to investors.
- Mutual funds are introducing flexible investment schedule.
- Mutual funds are providing greater affordability and liquidity.
- Mutual funds has simplified record keeping.
- It's support to capital market and money market.
- It is providing Industrial Development.
- Mutual funds acting as substitute for initial public offering.
- Mutual funds are reducing the market cost of new issues.
- It is keeping the money market active.

CHIT FUNDS

The chit is the most ingenious investment instrument, devised by mankind. A two-in-one, saving cum borrowing investment option. Evolved over 3,000 years. If possibly yielding the highest return on investor money.

QUESTIONS FOR DISCUSSIONS

1. Define the following:
   - Provident Fund
   - Statutory Provident Fund
   - Recognised Provident Fund
   - Public Provident Fund
   - Unrecognised Provident Fund
   - Units
   - Money Market Instruments
   - Treasury Bills
   - Certificate of Deposits
   - Commercial paper
   - REPOs
   - Bank deposits
   - Term Deposits
   - Precious Objects
   - LIC
   - Types of Policy
   - Endowment Policy
   - Term Policy
   - Money Back Plan Policy
   - Immediate Annuity Policy
   - Deferred Annuity Policy
   - Real Estate
   - Types of Residential Estate
   - Mutual Funds
   - Close End Funds
   - Open End Funds
   - Income Fund
   - Growth Fund

- Balance Fund
- Specialised Fund
- Money Market
- Taxation Fund
- Chit Funds

2. Briefly discuss the Provident Fund and its type.
3. What are the "feature of public provident fund"?
4. Describe the unit trust of India functions and objectives.
5. Explain the UTI schemes.
6. Describe the money market instrument and its feature and objectives.
7. Write a short note on the treasury bills.
8. What are the features of CDs?
9. Describe the advantages of CDs.
10. Describe the commercial papers feature and its advantages.
11. Explain the Bank Deposits.
12. Briefly write on precious objects.
13. Discuss about LIC and its objectives.
14. Explain the LIC as a investment.
15. What are the advantages of whole life policy?
16. Write briefly notes on Real Estate and its types.
17. What is mutual fund?
18. Discuss the different types of mutual fund.
19. What are the difference between open ended funds and close ended funds?
20. Briefly explain the importance of mutual fund.

REFERENCES

Bhole L.M., *Financial Institutions and Markets,* Tata McGraw Hill, New Delhi, 2004.

Prasanna Chandra, *Investment Analysis and Portfolio Management,* Tata McGraw Hill, 2003.

Prasanna Chandra, *Financial Management,* Tata McGraw Hill, New Delhi, 2004.

Jones C.P., *Investments: Analysis and Management,* Second Edition, John Wiley, New York, 1988.

Henning, Pigott, *Financial Markets and Economy,* Prentice Hall Inc., Englewood Cliffa, New Jersey, 1978.

Khan M.Y., *Indian Financial System: Theory and Practice,* Vikas Publishing House, New Delhi, 1989.

Murry E. Pallkot., *Financial Institutions and Markets,* Hughton Miffin Co., USA, 1970.

Website of UTI, LIC, RBI, SBI, Canara Bank, Birla Mutual Fund, HDFC, IDBI, ICICI etc.

Robinson R.I. and Wrightsman D., *Financial Markets,* McGraw Hill, International Book Co., London, 1981.

SEBI Annual Report

Verma J.L., *A Manual of Merchant Banking,* Bharat Law House, New Delhi, 1989.

Badger Tigeraon Guthman, *Investment Principles and Practices,* Prentici Hall, Englewood Cliffs, USA, 1969.

Christy and Clenderin, *An Introduction to Investments,* 7th Edition, McGraw Hill, USA, 1978.

RBI Bulletins

World Bank Report

Indian Companies Act 1956

■■■

CHAPTER 5

STOCK EXCHANGE

Learning Objectives

- Common people will be aware of stock exchange functions, powers and buying and selling of Securities.
- Who are Brokers? What is the role of Brokers? Explain the Double responsibility towards investors.
- We know the SEBI, Functions and Power.
- We know the Major limitations of Stock Exchange in India

INTRODUCTION

In this chapter, we shall outlook for:

- Stock Exchange functions, role, importance in dealing, service, power, bylaws and membership
- Listing of securities, advantages and disadvantages
- Trading in securities, operations, cleared and uncleared securities
- Stock broker, duties and types
- Speculation, types of speculator and speculative transactions
- National Stock Exchange and its features
- SEBI objectives, functions and power
- OTCEI objectives
- Impact of certain indicators on Stock Exchange

Meaning and Definition of Stock Exchange

A stock exchange is an organisation of brokers and investment bankers which has the purpose of providing the facilities for trade of company stocks and other financial instruments-usually a central location and record keeping. Trade on exchange is by members only. One is said to "have a seat" on the exchange. In Europe, stock exchanges are often called bourses. The trading of stock on stock exchanges is called the stock market.

Generally, stock exchange is a market in which securities are bought and sold and it is an essential component of a developed capital market.

According to the Securities Contracts (Regulation) Act 1956

Stock exchange means anybody of individuals, whether incorporated or not, constituted for the purpose of assisting, regulating or controlling the business of buying, selling or dealing in securities. According to this Act, securities include the following:

- Shares, scripts, stocks, bonds, debentures, stock or other marketable securities of any incorporated company or corporate
- Government securities
- Right or interest securities

Role and Importance of Stock Exchange

Exhibit 5.1 Role and importance of Stock Exchange

- The stock exchange will play an important role in the success of the economy of the country.
- The stock exchange is one of the basic financial tools for stimulating the economy by attracting capital for investment in the projects.
- The stock exchange also helps to revive other sectors of the economy such as commerce, industry and service.
- The stock exchange is attracting foreign capital to the country (India) particularly at present time, when the international companies have shown serious interest in the country as an important place for their investment.
- Shares, scrips, stocks, debentures stock and government securities are traded in stock exchange.
- Stock exchanges are provided appropriate advice to their clients.
- Stock exchange will list public private and foreign companies.
- Stock exchange wish to join the linkage system between the region's stock exchanges and at a latter stage, with international stock exchanges.
- Stock exchange is providing a market that mobilises and distributes the nation's savings utilised for the best purpose of the country.
- Stock exchange is a market in which securities are bought and sold.
- The opportunity for stock exchanges to render the services of stimulating private savings and channellising such savings into productive investment.

Functions of Stock Exchange

Exhibit 5.2 Functions of stock exchange

- A stock exchange is a very important financial market.
- Stock exchange is a highly efficient and visible instrument of financing.
- Stock exchange is used to finance the most of the needs of corporations, way of above financing available from banks.
- Individuals and firms save some of their income and invest it.
- The stock exchange is a meeting ground for savers wishing to invest their savings-and firms looking for investments.
- Another function of stock exchanges is to assist government in financing their internal borrowing requirements.
- Government sell obligations (called bonds) to investors through the stock exchanges in their countries.
- Stock exchange is an indispensable tool for refinancing national debt.
- Stock exchange is a market in which securities are bought and sold.
- Shares, scrips, stocks, debenture stocks and government securities are traded in stock exchange

Dealings on Stock Exchange

Dealing on the stock exchange are subject to the bylaws and rules of the stock exchange. Stock exchange dealings in India are regulated by the Securities Contracts (Regulation) Act. Stock exchange is permitted only in the listed securities through the members or their authorised clerks during the fixed working hours.

There are two important types of trading in the stock exchange:

- Ready Delivery Contract
- Forward Delivery Contract

Ready Delivery Contract

Ready delivery contract is also known as cash trading or cash transactions. These transactions are to be settled either on the same date or within a short period that may extend at the best up to seven days (If the payment and delivery of securities is on the same day or on the next day, it may be called spot delivery contract). Ready delivery contracts must be settled within the specified limit and they cannot be carried over to an extended period. Contracts can be made in respect of all securities.

Forward Delivery Contract

The forward delivery contracts are discharged on fixed settlement days occurring at fortnightly intervals. Forward delivery contracts enjoy the facility of 'carry-over'. Forward delivery contracts are confined to those securities which are planned on the forward list.

Difference between the Ready Delivery Contract and the Forward Delivery Contract

Exhibit 5.3 Differnce between the Ready Delivery Contract and Forward Delivery Contract

Ready Delivery Contract	*Forward Delivery Contract*
• Ready delivery contract also known as cash trading or cash transactions these are to be settled either on the same date or within a short period that may extend at the best up to seven days	• The Forward delivery contracts are discharged on fixed settlement days accruing fortnightly intervals
• Ready delivery contracts must be settled within the specified limit and they cannot be carried over to an extended period	• Forward delivery contracts enjoy the facility of 'carry over' to an extended period
• Ready delivery contracts can be made in respect of all securities	• Forward delivery contracts are confined to those securities which are placed on the forward list

SERVICE OF STOCK EXCHANGE

The stock market occupies a pivotal position in the financial system. It performs several economic functions and renders invaluable services to the investors, companies, and to the economy. The following are the services provided by the stock exchange.

- Liquidity and Marketability of Securities
- Safety of Funds
- Supply of Long Term Funds
- Flow of Capital to Profitable Ventures
- Motivation for Improved Performance
- Promotion of Investment
- Reflection of Business Cycle
- Marketing of New Issues
- Miscellaneous Services

Liquidity and Marketability of Securities

Stock exchanges provide buying and selling of securities. Stock exchange provide liquidity to securities since securities can be converted into cash at any time according to the discretion of investor by selling them at the listed price. This facility is providing continuous marketability to the investors in respect of securities they hold or intend to hold.

Safety of Funds

Over trading, illegitimate speculation etc. are prevented through carefully designed set of rules, regulations and the byelaws are meant to ensure safety of investible funds. Therefore, stock exchange is protected investors fund.

Supply of Long Term Funds

In security market, securities are transferable from one person to another with minimum formalities. When security is sold, one investor is substituted by another. However, the company is assured availability of long term funds.

Flow of Capital to Profitable Venture

The profitability and popularity of companies are reflected in terms of hike in stocks. According to Husband and Dockeray "Stock exchanges function like a traffic signal, indicating a green light when certain fields offer the necessary inducement to attract capital blazing a red light when the outlook for new investments is not attractive."

Motivation for Improved Performance

The performance of a company is reflected in terms of prices quoted in the stock market. Stock exchange always encourages to improve performance of companies. Because public can expect to invest in growth companies.

Promotion of Investment

Stock exchanges mobilise the savings from the public into effective production purpose. In this way, stock exchange can promote investment through capital formation.

Reflection of Business Cycle

The changing economic and business conditions are immediately reflected on the stock exchanges. Stock exchange identifies the booms and depressions of the economy. The government can take suitable monetary and fiscal policies which can help to investors.

Marketing of New Issues

If the new issues are listed in stock exchange. Stock exchanges ready to accept and their evaluation by concerned stock exchange authorities. Stock market always helps in marketing of new issues.

Miscellaneous Issues

Stock exchange encourages public to mobilise their savings. It guides investors in choosing securities by supplying the daily quotation of list of securities. It exhibits recent trends of the companies in the business.

History of Stock Exchange

In India, the only stock exchanges operated in the 19th century were those of Mumbai in 1875 and Ahmedabad setup in 1894. Both stock exchanges were organised as voluntary nonprofit making associations of brokers. The main intention and objectives is to regulate and protect their interests. Bombay Securities Control Act 1925, which was recognised the Bombay Stock Exchange in 1937 and Ahmedabad in 1937. During the war period, a number of stock exchanges were organised even in Mumbai, Ahmedabad and other centers, therefore, they were not recognised. After the Independence the Central Government was passed the Securities Contracts Regulation Act in 1956 in Parliament.

Powers of Central Government

Exhibit 5.4 Power of Central Government

Powers of Central Government under Securities Contracts Regulation Act 1956, as outlined below:

- Grant and withdraw of recognition of stock exchanges, approval or change of buylaws
- Call for periodical yield from the stock exchange
- Direct enquiries is relating to the members of the stock exchange
- Stock exchanges are submitted annual reports to Government
- Central Government is making certain rules which relating to stock exchange operation
- Supersede and suspend the Governing Board of Exchange
- Government ready to impose any other conditions or regulations for trading

BYELAWS

The Securities Contracts (Regulation) Act 1956 to regulate certain matters such as:

- Opening/closing of stock exchanges
- Administration timing of trading
- Regulation of blank transfers
- Regulation of Badla or carry over business
- Control of the settlement and other activities
- The stock exchange
- Fixation of margins
- Fixation of market size
- Regulation of business
- Regulation of brokers traders
- Brokerage charges
- Trading rules on the stock exchange
- Arbitration and settlement of disputes
- Settlement and clearing of the trading etc.

Relating to trading on the stock exchanges. These are known as byelaws of the Exchanges.

Present Recognised Stock Exchange

At present, there are 23 stock exchanges recognised under the Securities Contracts (Regulation) Act 1956. They are located at:

- Mumbai
- Calcutta
- Chennai
- Delhi
- Ahmedabad
- Hyderabad
- Indore
- Bhuwaneshwar
- Mangalore
- Patna
- Bangalore
- Rajkot
- Guwahati
- Jaipur

- Kanpur
- Ludhiana
- Baroda
- Cochin
- Pune
- Coimbatore
- Meerut
- Vishakapatnam
- Vijayawada

Qualifications for Membership

Exhibit 5.5 Qualifications for Membership

The member of a recognised stock exchange, a person must possess the following qualification:

- He should be citizen of India and his age is not less than 21 years
- He should not have been insolvent or bankrupt
- He should not have been convicted for fraud or dishonesty
- He should have the educational qualifications 10+2
- He should not connected with a company or corporation
- He should not a defaulter of any other stock exchange

ORGANISATION STRUCTURE OF STOCK EXCHANGE

The organisation structure of stock exchanges are different from place to place. Different forms are:

- Voluntary non-profit making association - 3 Stock Exchanges
- Public Limited Company - 14 Stock Exchanges
- Company Limited by Guarantee - 6 Stock Exchanges

Mumbai, Ahmedabad and Indore are three recognised Stock Exchanges. These are the voluntary non-profit making associations.

Calcutta, Delhi, Bangalore, Cochin, Kanpur, Ludhiana, Guwahati Stock Exchanges are the examples of Public Limited Company/Joint Stock Companies Limited by Shares.

Hyderabad, Mumbai and Pune Stock Exchanges are the examples of the Companies Limited by Guarantee.

LISTING OF SECURITIES

Listing of securities means the securities are admission for trading on a recognised stock exchange. In the case of securities are not listed in the stock exchange such company securities are not trading in the stock exchange.

Listing is compulsory for a public issuing company that intend to offer shares/debentures to the public for subscription. Listed securities are of two classes, viz., cash List and Forward List. The securities on the cash list are those involving ready delivery while securities in the forward list enjoy forward trading privileges.

Advantages of Listing

Exhibit 5.6 Advantages of Listing

Listing has some advantages

- Listing of securities provides the marketability and liquidity of the securities
- Listing protects the interest of both shareholders and the investing public
- Listing encourages investment and flow of savings into the capital market
- Listing offers wide publicity to the concerned companies
- Listing provides buying and selling of securities in the stock exchange
- Listing promotes better corporate practices and lead to progressively higher standards of corporate procedures and practices
- Listing enjoys higher public confidence as the stock exchange compels the issuer to comply with high standards.

Disadvantages of Listing

Exhibit 5.7 Disadvatages of Listing

- Listed securities offers wide scope for the speculators to manipulate the values in such a way as detrimental to the interest of the company
- Sometime listed securities are subject to wide fluctuations in their value. The wide fluctuations in their values have the effect of degrading the company's reputation and images in the eyes of the public as well as the financial intermediaries
- Listing discloses vital information such as operating environment to competitors.

TRADING IN SECURITIES

The Securities Contracts (Regulation) Act 1956 is the special tool for regulation of securities contracts and the Stock Exchanges in India. It was passed in 1956 and came into force on February 20, 1957. It regulated the trading in securities on the stock exchanges and options trading and enhance for recognition of stock exchanges and relating matters like in terms of listing of securities, transfer of securities, etc. The trading in securities which is governed by the Rules and Byelaws of the Stock Exchange.

Meaning of Securities

According to the Securities Contracts (Regulation) Act 1956, Section 2(h) defines the key word "Securities". Securities includes shares, scrips, stocks, bonds, debentures, debenture stock or other marketable securities of a like nature in or of any incorporated company or other body corporate. Securities also covers government securities and rights or interests in securities. But it does not include securities of private companies as they are not capable of being dealt in on a stock exchange and are not marketable securities due to possible restrictions on transfer. The major instruments in securities trading such as debentures, public sector bonds and government securities.

Issue of Securities

Issue of securities are as outlined below:

- Government Securities
- Corporate Securities
- Corporate Debentures
- Company Deposits
- Commercial Paper
- Fixed Deposits
- Equity Shares
- Preference Shares
- Bonds

These are various alternative issues of primary securities.

STOCK MARKET OPERATIONS

Equity shares, Preference shares, Debentures, Government Securities, Bonds these are listed according to the Securities Contracts (Regulation) Rules, 1957 and the Byelaws of the stock exchange. These securities are listed for trading automatically after they are issued to the public without any listing fees.

Cleared and Non-Cleared Securities

The listed securities are generally classified into two categories namely:

- Group A Shares (Specified Shares or Cleared Securities)
- Group B Shares (Non-specified Shares or Non-cleared Securities)

Group A shares/Specified shares or Cleared Securities represent large and well established companies having a broad investor base. Specified shares/securities list should be fully paid up equity shares listed already on the Stock Exchange. The company must have a record of good earnings and dividends over the past few years. These shares/ securities are actively traded and facility for carrying forward a transaction from one account period to another is available. Naturally, specified shares/cleared securities attract a lot of speculative multiples. These facilities are not available to Group B Shares/Non-specified Shares/non-cleared securities. Therefore, shares can be moved from Group B to Group A and vice versa depending upon the criteria for shifting. Furthermore, to specified/cleared/A Group and non-specified/not cleared/B Group are not listed on that exchange but listed on some other exchange, but permitted to be traded here.

STOCK BROKER

Stock Broker

- An agent that charges a fee or commission for executing buy and sell orders submitted by an investor
- The firm that acts as an agent for a customer, charging the customer a commission for its service
- A stock broker is someone who performs transactions on the stock market on behalf of third parties who are unable or unwilling to trade themselves
- Stock broker who is a member of the stock exchange to deal securities on recognised stock exchanges, the broker should register his name as a broker with the SEBI. A stock broker should possess the following qualifications to register as a broker.
- He should be an Indian Citizen within 21 years of age
- He should not be bankrupt or compounded with creditors
- He should not have been convicted for any offence, fraud etc.
- He should not have engaged in any other business other than that of a broker in securities
- He should not be defaulter of any stock exchange
- He should have completed 12th Standard examination.

Apart from Individuals, Corporate and Institutional members can also be become brokers. Brokers will be selected by the Selection Committee of the Stock Exchange on the basis of their qualifications, experience, financial status, their performance in the written text, interview etc.

Duties/Code of Conduct for Stock Brokers

Duties are discharged in the best interest of Investors, and other stock broker, A code of conduct which in prescribed for brokers in accordance with the statutory requirements. They have been briefly outlined as below:

- A stock broker should be honest and promptly execute all orders regarding upon buying and selling of securities. He should make prompt payment to his clients in the case of sales and prompt delivery in the case of purchases.
- He should not difference between small investors and big investors.
- He should issue a contract note for all transactions as specified by the stock exchange without any delay.
- He should maintain complete secrecy of his client's personal investment and other informations of a confidential nature.
- He should not influence purchases or sales just for the sake of his brokerage or commission.
- He should not give any false and misleading information to his clients particularly as relating to sales and purchases of securities.
- He should not entertain those clients who have failed to carry out their commitments in respect of securities with other stock brokers.
- He should acting as duly informed to his client.
- He should have adequate infrastructure facilities and maintain proper staff to render prompt, efficient and fair service to his clients.
- He should not advertise his business publicly except when it is permitted by the stock exchange.
- He should not adopt unfair practices with a view to attracting clients from other brokers.
- He should not fail to submit the necessary returns to the SEBI.

- He should exercise reasonable care, diligence and skill in the discharge of his functions as a broker.
- He should abide by all the rules and regulations of the regulating authorities even included the stock exchange.
- He must maintain proper books of account, records and documents which are required by the various regulating authorities.
- He must produce the above books and records for inspection whenever an inspection is undertaken as per the provisions of the SEBI Act.

REGISTRATION OF SUB-BROKERS

A sub-broker is not a member of a stock exchange. Therefore, he is a person who acts as an agent of a stock broker. He undertakes the securities trading business on behalf of his clients by through stock brokers. Sub-brokers should also get a certificate of registration from SEBI. Just like as brokers, they have to satisfy the eligibility criteria, pay registration fees and follow the code of conduct and the various rules and regulations framed by the regulating authorities from time to time. In this case excepting the registration fees, other aspects are more or less similar to brokers.

Types/Kinds of Brokers

Brokers may be classified as outlined below:

- Jobbers
- Commission Broker
- Tarawaniwalas
- Sub-brokers/Remisers
- Floor Broker
- Odd Lot Dealer
- Budliwala
- Arbitrageur
- Dealers in Non-cleared Securities
- Security Dealer
- Authorised Clerk

Jobbers

A Jobber is a professional and independent broker who deals in securities on his behalf. It means, he purchases and sells securities in his own name. His main job objective is to earn a margin of profit due to price variations of securities. Jobbers is a professional broker who carefully judges the value of the securities and makes a good forecast of their future price movements. He buys securities as a owner, keeps them for a very short period and sells them for profit known as the Jobber's turn.

A Jobber will always quote a two-way price called double-barreled price. The lower price indicate that the jobber is ready to purchase and higher price indicate that the jobber is ready to sell the securities.

Commission Brokers

A commission broker is nothing but a broker. He buys and sells securities for earning a commission on behalf of the clients. He is permitted to deal with non-members directly. His main function is to buy and sell securities on behalf of his client and earning commission. He does not purchase or sell in his name.

Tarawaniwalas

A Tarawaniwala is an active member in the stock exchange. He is similar to as Jobber. Tarawaniwalas act as a broker and as well as a jobber. He is not prohibited from acting as a broker. This system demerit is that a tarawaniwala can act against the interest of investors by purchasing securities from them in his own name at lower prices and selling the same securities to them at higher prices.

Sub-broker

As stated earlier, a sub-broker is an agent of a stock broker. He helps the clients to buy and sell securities only through the stock broker.

Floor Broker

Floor brokers are not found on Indian Stock Exchanges. The floor broker buys and sells shares for other brokers on the floor of exchange. The floor brokers are not officially attached to other members. The floor broker executes orders for any members and receives as his compensation a share of brokerage charged by the commission.

Odd Lot Dealer

The odd lot dealer specialises in buying and selling in amount less than the prescribed trading units or lots. He buys odd lots and makes them upto marketing trading units or lots. He engaged in round lot transactions. The price of the odd lot is determined by the round lot transactions. He earns high profit on the difference between the price at which he buys and sells the securities. He does not rely on commission.

Buddiwala

Buddiwala is a financier in the stock exchange. He is also known as Budliwalla. He is giving credit facilities to the market. And he charge a fee which called as 'Contango' or 'Backwardation' charge. He gives a secured loan that for a short period of two to three weeks. The return is governed by technical position of the market and ruling the rate of interest.

Arbitrageur

Arbitrageur is a specialist in buying and selling in securities in different markets at the same time and profits by the difference in the price between the two stock exchanges.

Dealers in Non-cleared Securities

He is a specialist in buying and selling on his own account shares which are not in the active list.

Security Dealer

He is a specialist in buying and selling the Government or Gilt Edge securities.

Authorised Clerks

An authorised clerk is one who is appointed by a stock broker to assist him in the business of securities trading. As per the rules of the stock exchange, each broker can employ a specified number of authorised clerks to transact the securities trading business.

Kind/Types of Transaction in a Stock Exchange

The Stock Exchanges are permitted to the members on behalf of his client to enter into transactions in securities as outlined.

- Spot delivery
- Hand delivery
- Special delivery

Spot Delivery

Means for delivery and payment on the same day.

Hand Delivery

Means for delivery and payment with the time, which shall not more than 14 days.

Special Delivery

For delivery and payment within any time exceeding 14 days following the date of contract as may be stipulated when entering into the bargain and permitted by the governing board.

BADLA TRANSACTION/CARRY OVER

Badla transaction/carry over refers to the postponement of the settlement of transaction till the next settlement period. It is a facility to carry forward the transaction from one settlement period to another. If the buyers/sellers wish to carry forward their transactions from settlement period to the next settlement period, they draw up a fresh set of contract notes to give effect to the carry forward of the purchase/sale at rates which reflect the badla charges.

Badla Charges

Badla charges are fixed on the basis of demand and supply conditions in the market and they are fixed on a fortnightly basis. Therefore, the Badla charges could vary in different settlement periods. The carry forward charges or interest is to be paid by the buyer or seller in each scrip sold. Badla charges or the amount of interest charges is also known as Vyaj Badla.

Factors Influencing Badla Rates

The Badla charges or the amount of interest charges which are contracted to be paid as a result of carry forward the transaction from one settlement period to another are based on several factors as outlines below:

- The total amount of badla finance available in the market
- The speculative business position in the market
- Availability of badla finance for a particular scrip (scrip means speculative transaction)
- The present interest rates in the money market
- The psychological state of the market.

Speculation on the Stock Exchange

Speculation transactions are made with the intention of making profits by disposing of securities at favourable prices. Speculative transactions does not involve full payment for and taking delivery of the securities which the speculators have contracted to transfer. Speculators do not take/give delivery of shares. They deal in differences in the purchase and sale prices. Their main intention is to carry forward the transactions and get short term gains due to price differences.

Kinds/Types of Speculators

Speculators of the stock exchanges may be classified into the three. They are as outlined below:

- Bull
- Bear
- Stag

Bull

A Bull is also known as Tejwalla, Bulls are very optimistic of the rise in prices of securities. He is a speculator who buys shares in the expectation of selling it at a higher price latter. Thus, in a bull market there will be excess of purchases over sales.

Bear

A bear is also known as Mandiwalla. Bears are very pessimistic and always they expect a fall in the prices of securities in future. Hence, Bear goes on selling securities. Therefore, a bearish market refers to a falling market and there will be excess sales over purchases.

Stag

A stag neither buys nor sells but applies for subscription to the new issues expecting that he can sell them at a premium. Generally, Stag buys new issues and sell it on allotments or even before allotment for a profit.

SPECULATIVE TRANSACTIONS

Speculative transactions are:

- Option Dealing
- Wash Sales
- Arbitrage
- Cornering
- Rigging the Market
- Blank Transfers
- Margin Trading

Option Dealing

Option is the right to buy or sell a certain quantity of security at a certain price within a certain time. The option to buy is known as call option or Teji Sauda and the option to sell is known as Put Option/ Mandi Sauda. The Put and Call is q double option (known as Teji Mandi) giving right either to purchase or to sell securities. In an option dealing, a speculator is given the right or option to buy or sell, or both buy and sell as the case may be on the settlement day or else he will forfeit the option money.

Wash Sales

It is technique through which a speculator is able to earn huge profits by creating a misleading picture in the market. It is of fictitious transaction in which a speculator sells and buys security at a higher price through another broker. However, it creates a false or misleading opinion in the market about the price of the security in question. As a result of misleading, the price records a further rise and the speculator is able to get high profits by selling the securities to the public. It is purely in the interest of speculators.

Arbitrage

Arbitrage is a highly skilled speculative activity. Arbitrage is a device to make profit out of the differences in prices of a security in two different markets. Arbitrages refers to carry of a security from one market to another, it is also described as traffic in securities. Such a traffic may be carried on between two markets with in the country is known as domestic arbitrage. A traffic may be carried on between two markets with one country to another country is known as Foreign Arbitrage.

Cornering

Cornering refers to the process of holding the entire supply securities by an individual or a group of individuals in terms to the short sellers and earning more profits. In this case, the short sellers (i.e., bears) who have contracted to sell the security without actually possessing it would be unable to deliver it to the buyers, who have cornered the market. It is also a prohibited activity.

Rigging the Market

Rigging is the process to create an artificial condition in the market. This impact is the price fluctuation of the securities in the market. Speculators main intention is earning of huge profit from the speculation.

Blank Transfers

Blank transfer helps to speculative activities by through carry-over/ badla transactions. The transferror (seller) signs the transfer form without specifying the name of the transferee (buyer) as known as blank transfer. Badla/carryover transactions are involves temporary purchases and sales of securities.

Blank transfer is an undesirable activity due to the following reasons:

- In the case of partly paid up capital, the seller's liability is continues even after he actually sold it. It is not justifiable.
- Blank transferee escapees from the payment of stamp duty and transfer fees etc. which is the loss of revenue to the government.
- In the case of blank transfer, the transferee's name is not disclosed. Therefore, he can evade income tax.
- Blank transferees to gain control of the management of companies without disclosing their names.
- The blank transferee's name will not be recorded in the register of companies. Therefore, the registers are incomplete and misleading information to perspective investors.
- Registered shares are made freely negotiable through blank transfers. However, it encourages unhealthy speculation.

Margin Trading

Margin Trading is a popular method of Speculative Trading. In this method, the client opens an account with his broker. Client makes deposit of cash or securities in his account. Client has agreed to maintain a minimum margin of amount deposit always in his account. When, broker purchases securities on behalf of his client his account will be debited and vice versa.

NATIONAL STOCK EXCHANGE OF INDIA

The National Stock Exchange of India (NSEI) was established in 1994 to encourage stock exchange reform through system modernisation and competition. It is an electronic screen based system where members have equal access and equal opportunity of business irrespective of their location in different parts of the country as they are connected through a satellite network.

The National Stock Exchange is to operate in two segments as outlined below:

- Wholesale Debt Market
- Capital Market

Wholesale Debt Market is concerned with trading instruments such as Gilt edge securities, commercial papers, PSU Bonds, units, and certificate of Deposits.

The Capital Market is concerned with equity and corporate debt instruments.

Objectives of National Stock Exchange

The NSE objectives as outlined below:

- It establishes nation wide trading facility for equity debt and hybrid.
- It facilitates equal access to investors across the country.
- It provides fairness, efficiency and transparency to the securities trading.
- It enables shorter settlement cycles.
- It meets international securities market standard.

Features of NSE

- It set up a fully automated screen based trading system
- It has consists of three segments: The capital market segment, wholesale debt market segment and derivatives market
- It market is a fully automated screen based environment
- It own's satellite network by through market operates with all participants stationed at their office and making use of their computer terminals, to receive market information, to enter orders and execute to trade.
- The NSE has opted for an order driven system.

This system provides enormous flexibility to trading members. A trading member can place various conditions on the order in terms of price, time or size when an order is placed by a trading member, an order confirmation slip is generated. All orders received are staked in price and time priority. The computer system automatically reaches for a match and no sooner to the same is found the deal is struck.

- When a trade take place, a trade confirmation slip is printed at the trading member's work station.

It gives detail like price/quantity, code number of the party and so on.

- It pending orders is delayed, the identity of the trading is not revealed to others.

- On the eighth day of trading, each member get a statement showing his net position as the clearing house of the securities.
- Members are required to deliver securities and cash by the thirteenth and fourteenth day respectively, the fifteenth day is the payout day.
- It automated trade matching system secures the best prices available in the market to the investor.

SECURITIES AND EXCHANGE BOARD OF INDIA

The Securities and Exchange Board of India (SEBI) was established on April 12, 1988 under a resolution of the Government of India. But, it was latter made a statutory body by the Securities and Exchange Board of India Act 1992. According to this Act, the SEBI shall typically consist of a chairman and five other members appointed by the Central Government (Two members representing the ministries of finance and law, one member from the Reserve Bank of India and two other members).

With came into effect of the Securities and Exchange Board of India Act 1992, powers and functions exercised by the Central Government with respect of the regulation of the stock exchange operations in India.

Objectives of SEBI

Exhibit 5.8 **Objectives of SEBI**

- To protect the interest of Investors
- To regulate the securities market
- To promote efficient services by brokers merchant bankers and other intermediaries

Functions of SEBI

Exhibit 5.9 **Functions of SEBI**

I. Regulatory Functions:

- Regulation of stock exchange and any other security market
- Registration and regulation of working stock brokers, subbrokers, registrar to all issue, merchant bankers, under writers, portfolio managers and such other intermediaries who are associated with securities market
- Registration and regulation of the working of collective investment including mutual funds

contd...

- Prohibition of prudulent and unfair trade practices relating to securities market
- Prohibit insider trading in securities
- Regulating substantial acquisitions of shares and take over of companies

II. Developmental Functions:

- Promote Investor's education
- Training of intermediaries
- Conducting research and its information useful to all market participants
- Promotion of pair practice and code of conduct for self regulatory organisations.

Powers of SEBI

Exhibit 5.10 Powers of SEBI

SEBI vests the following powers:

- Power to call periodical return from recognised stock exchanges
- Power to call any information or explanation from recognised stock exchanges or their members
- Power to direct enquiries to be made in relation to affairs of stock exchanges or their members
- Power to grant approval to byelaws of recognised stock exchanges
- Power to make or amend byelaws of recognised stock exchanges
- Power to compel listing of securities of public companies
- Power to control and regulate stock exchanges
- Power to grant registration to market intermediaries
- Power to levy fees or other charges for carrying out the purpose of regulation
- Power to declare applicability of Section 17 of the Securities Contract (Regulation) Act is any area to grant licences to dealers in securities.

OVER THE COUNTER EXCHANGE OF INDIA (OTCEI)

Over the counter market is a market where buyers seek out sellers and vice versa and then attempt to arrange terms and conditions for purchase/sale acceptable to both parties. In OTC refers trading take place by putting buy and sell orders by telephone, telex, letter, oral message, etc. There is no particular market place in the geographical area.

Basic Objectives of OTC

Basic objective of OTC are as outlined below:

- Quicker liquidity
- Fixed and Fair Price

- Liquidity for a less trade security or it suited to small company
- Simplified process of buying and selling
- Creation of public interest in risky, although viable ventures
- Easy of making public sale of new issues.

OTCEI

The OTCEI was incorporated in 1990 as a company under the Companies Act 1956. It became fully operational on September 1992, with opening of a counter in Bombay. The OTCEI is recognised by the Government of India as a recognised Stock Exchange under Section 4 of the Securities Control Regulation Act, 1956.

Promoters

The OTCEI has been promoted by all financial institutions in India such as UTI, ICICI, IDBI, IFCI, LIC, GID, SBI Capital Markets, etc.

Benefits to the Investors

The OTC Exchange offers a number of benefits to the investors. They are as mentioned below:

- Quick payment of money to the sellers and quick delivery of shares to buyers
- Price transparency means buyer and seller know the actual price at which the scrips are bought or sold for him in other stock exchanges
- The OTCEI saves the investors from other unscrupulous behaviour of the brokers
- Liquidity even for scrips of small and new companies
- Fair prices
- Simple procedure of buying and selling
- Facility to sell even odd lots.

Benefits to the Companies

The OTC exchange offers certain benefits to the companies. The benefits are outlined below:

- It enables even smaller and less liquid companies to get listed
- Facilitate new issues at lower cost
- Market raising capital through issues easy for small, new and closely held companies
- Helps create market for scrips of small and new companies.

Impact of Certain Economic Indicators on Stock Exchange/ Limitations of Indian Stock Market

The Indian Stock Market has suffered from many limitations. An important limitations are outlines below:

- Absence of genuine investors
- Presence of price rigging
- Prevalence of Insider Trading
- Lack of liquidity
- Scarcity of floating securities
- Lack of transparency
- Poor response of Indian Households
- High volatility of stock market
- Cumbersome procedures of settlement
- Problem of odd lots
- Dominance of financial institution
- Lack of professionalism
- Dominance of public sector
- Unhealthy competition of merchant bankers
- Other defects.

These factors are the major impact of certain economic indicators on stock exchange.

Absence of Genuine Investors

Speculative activities are created absence of genuine investors. Therefore, speculators always earn more profit from buying and selling of securities in the securities market. Most of the transactions are carry forward transactions with a speculative motive of deriving benefit from short term fluctuations.

Lack of Transparency

SEBI has regulated stock exchanges in India. But unable to regulate the stock market operations brokers and speculators. Many brokers and speculators are violating rules and regulations with a view to cheating to the customers in the market.

High Volatility of Stock Market

Research survey has indicated that the high price fluctuations in the capital market. The high price volatility is not good for smooth functioning of the stock market.

Problem of Odd Lots

Odd lots means tradable securities are not listed in the market. This is the major problem to the security holders. It discourage to the trading activities to the investor.

Dominance of Financial Institutions

Financial institutions like LIC, UTI, GIC are dominated in the stock market. In additionally, these are majority influence and control in the securities market in stock exchange.

Lack of Professionalism

Professionals are efficiently managed and Administration of the security operations. The lack of the professionalism has been creating several problems to investors, brokers and speculators. Professionals are aware of the financial institution role in the operation market. If lack, a problems for brokers and their clients.

Presence of Price Rigging

There is a strong bull moment in a market has created artificially demand for the products and push up the prices before the issues of securities. This process has generally done by a few group involved in buying and selling of the securities.

Prevalence of Insider Trading

Insider Trading has been practice has been accepted in India. Although, the SEBI has introduced many regulations to control the insider trading. Insider means insider are those who have access to unpublished price-sensitive information by virtue of their good position in the company and who ready to use such information in their best merits.

Lack of Liquidity

Around 8000 companies are listed in Stock Exchanges in India. The shares of only a few companies are actively traded in the market and become they are liquid. Remaining shares of the listed companies are not actively traded in the market and become they are lack of liquidity.

Scarcity of Floating Securities

In the stock market, there is a scarcity of floating securities. The security market is highly volatile and easy price manipulations. In additionally, there is inadequate supply of good scrips and imbalance of demand and supply of securities in the market.

Dominance of Public Sector

In recent trends, the investors are lost faith in Private Sector. However, the private sector has been having a little success in equity mobilisation.

Unhealthy Competition of Merchant Bankers

Around 800 merchant bankers rendering their services in the capital market. Merchant Bankers participants are increased. Its impact is to led unhealthy competition and dilution of the quality of services.

Other Defects

Other defects are:

- Investors apathy due to their loss of confidence
- Delay in refund of the application money issuing of allotment letters, posting of share certificate etc.
- Bad delivers

These are factors are impacts on Indian Economy and major defects of Capital Market.

QUESTIONS FOR DISCUSSION

1. Define the following:
    - Stock Exchange
    - Ready Delivery Contract
    - Forward Delivery Contract
    - Byelaws
    - Listing of Securities
    - Securities
    - Cleared Securities
    - Noncleared Securities
    - Brokers
    - Jobbers
    - Tarawaniwalas
    - Floor Broker
    - Odd Lot Dealer
    - Badliwala
    - Arbitrager
    - Badla Charges

- Bull
- Bear
- Stag
- Blank Transfer
- National Stock Exchange of India
- SEBI
- OTCEI

2. Discuss the role and importance of stock exchange.
3. Briefly explain the function and dealing of stock exchange.
4. Discuss the listing of securities. What are the advantages and disadvantages of the listing of securities?
5. Describe cleared and noncleared securities.
6. Discuss the types of broker.
7. Discuss the Badla Transactions.
8. Discuss the National Stock Exchange of India.
9. Describe the SEBI functions, objectives.
10. Briefly explain the OTCEI.
11. Describe the economic impact on stock exchange.

REFERENCES

Bhole L.M., *Financial Institutions and Markets,* Tata McGraw Hill, New Delhi, 2006.

Bombay Stock Exchange, Stock Exchange Directory.

Bangalore Stock Exchange, Stock Exchange Directory.

Gupta U.L., *Working of Stock Exchange of India,* Thompson Press, New Delhi, 1972.

SEBI Reports

CHAPTER

6 FUNDAMENTAL ANALYSIS OF INVESTMENT MANAGEMENT

Learning Objectives

- We shall know fundamental Analysis in the following terms:
  - Economic Analysis
  - Industry Analysis
  - Company Analysis
  - Financial Statement Analysis
  - Ratio Analysis
  - Cost Benefit Analysis
  - Risk Analysis

INTRODUCTION

- Investment management involves correct decision making of the buying or selling of the securities in the market.
- Investment management is risky and difficult to manage by the ordinary people.
- Investment management refers to decision making at risky and difficult movement in the market.
- Investment management is managed in terms of economic factors, industry analysis and company analysis. Soon after investment management is implementation of the decision regarding investment by investor.
- Investment is to aware of the market expectations and fluctuations in the secondary market.

What is Investment Management?

- Investment management refers to decision to buy or sell the securities in the market.
- Investment management decisions are influenced by the availability of money and flow of the money.
- Investment management is to study clearly about the valuation of shares. It means shares present value or it is under estimated or over estimated in the market.
- Common investors to know to will get first hand information about the fundamental analysis of the company in terms of company analysis, industry analysis and finally economic analysis. Common investors are forget to the Technical analysis of the company shares, securities, bonds etc. This study is comes under investment management.
- Investment management is to analyse the investment either short term or long term investment.
- Speculation is inevitable to the investment management.
- Investment management is to protect genuine investors against wrong timing of buying or selling securities in the market.
- Investment management decisions are scientific and rational that influence to take accurate decisions by the investors.
- Investment management is measure to high risk and low risk situations in the market.
- Investors are ready to refer about the company's balance sheet, annual reports, mission and goals. It gives clear picture of the industry. This reference has further helpful to investor to take decisions.

PROCEDURE AND CRITERIA FOR INVESTMENT DECISIONS

Procedure and criteria for investment decisions depends on the mood of the market. As per the research studies show that shares prices depend on the company's performance basis of past, present and future. Company's future is obvious from the point of view of the investor for investment. Investor's always desire to invest in the long term benefits oriented companies. Because they yield good return from the investing companies. Therefore, they are ability to forecast to performance of the company. Most of the investors are desired to invest in growth oriented companies.

The second procedure and criteria for investment decisions involves several factors as outlined below:

- Past performance
- Present working conditions of the company
- Present yield of the company
- Future expectation of the company
- Company's performance in terms of operations and financially

Above mentioned these factors can influence to the share price of the company.

Thirdly, the investment decision depends on the investor's perception on whether the present share price is fair, over valued or under valued. If the share price is fair, it will hold it (Hold Decision). If it is over valued, he will sell it (Sell Decision) and if it is under valued, he will buy it (Buy Decision). Thus even when prices are raising, some investors may buy as their expectations of further rise may outweigh his conception of over valuation. It means, the concept of over valuation or under valuation are relative to time, space and man, what may be overvalued or little while ago has become undervalued following later developments. Information or sentiment and mood may change the whole market scenario and of the valuation of shares.

The investors decision about the investment may also be their moods, preferences or fancies. The investors are careful about their investment. For example, if he has lack of information, he invested of company's performance reduce that ultimate result is price of shares reduced in the market, so his negligence is to loss his wealth in terms of investment. A rational investor would however make investment decisions on scientific study of the fundamentals of the company and in a planned manner.

At present, investor mostly depend on hear say and advice from friends, relatives, sub-brokers and family members etc. for the investment decision. Therefore, they are not considered any scientific study of the company's fundamentals. From the point of view of the increasing mushroom growth of companies and lack of any track record of money promoters, investment decision making has become more difficult now. Even otherwise, risk will increase in the case of all investments made on hunches, hear say etc.

RISK UNDER INVESTMENT MANAGEMENT

Risk can be defined as the chance that the expected or prospective advantage, gain, profit or return may not materialise that the actual outcome of investment may be less than the expected outcome. The greater the variability or dispersion of the possible outcomes, or the broader the range of possible outcomes, the greater the risk. Risk suggest that the decision maker knows that there is some possible consequence of an investment decision, but uncertainty involves a situation, where the outcome is not known to the decision maker. But basically, investment involve both risk and uncertainty. The word risk used to consist of all elements certainty, uncertainty, variability of the return and income.

Types of Risk

There are a number of sources or factors behind risk and depending upon the source. The following are the major types of risk:

- Default Risk
- Financial Risk
- Liquidity Risk
- Maturity Risk
- Call Risk
- Interest Rate Risk
- Inflation Risk
- Exchange Rate or Currency Risk
- Business Risk
- Total Risk
- Country Risk

Default Risk

Default risk arises from the failure on the part of the borrower or debtor to pay the specified amount of interest or to repay the principal or both. It means not only the complete failure to pay but also the delay in payments.

Financial Risk

Financial risk is associated with the use of debt financing by companies. Since the presence of debt involves the legal or must to make specified payments at specified time periods. The risk of the firm is earning is not sufficient to meet their requirement. Usually, financial risk is measured by the debt/equity ratio of the firm.

Liquidity Risk

Liquidity refers to a situation wherein it may not be possible to dispose off or sell the asset. A asset can be bought and sold quickly and without significant price concession and transaction cost is said to be liquid. Liquidity risk refers to their inability to meet the liabilities towards depositors when they want to withdraw their deposits.

Maturity Risk

Maturity risk arises when the term of maturity of the security which happens to be longer. The long investment has involving risk. The longer the term maturity that the greater the risk.

Call Risk

Call risk is associated with the corporate bonds that are issued with call back provisions. If such bonds, the bond holders is faced the risk of giving up higher coupon bonds.

Interest Rate Risk

Interest rate risk is the variability in return on security due to changes in the level of market interest rates, when the interest rates rise, the value of the security drops, and vice versa. The interest risk directly related to the length of time to maturity of security.

Inflation Risk

It is risk that the real return on a security may be less than the nominal return. Inflation risk is known as purchasing power risk. Inflation risk is based on the increased the price of commodities and decrease the price of commodities. This result comes on securities price. Inflation risk is closely related to interest rate risk.

Exchange Rate or Currency Risk

Currency risk refers to cash flow variability experienced by economic units engaged in international transactions or international exchange, on account of unexpected changes in exchange rates. Changes in currency rates may have an unfavourable impact on revenues of business.

Business Risk

Business risk is the uncertainty of income flows by the nature of a firm's business. Business risk causes from internal and external factors of the business.

Systematic Risk

Systematic risk refers to that portion of the total variability of the return caused by common factors affecting the prices of all securities in the market in terms of economic, political and social factors.

Examples of systematic risk:

- Market risk - Fluctuations in market conditions
- Interest rate risk - Fluctuations in interest rates

- Purchasing power - Inflation risk
- Trade cycles or Business conditions or monsoon rains based on Indian economy

Unsystematic Risk

Unsystematic risk refers to that to portion of the total variability of the return caused due to unique factors, which relating to that firms or industry in terms of management failure, labour strikes, raw material scarcity etc.

Examples of unsystematic risk:

- Business risk related to the industries
- Financial risk due to heavy interest burden for inefficient management
- Management risk arises due to poor efficiency, faulty planning
- Labour and other inputs risks relating to the company.

Unsystematic risk is also called as non-market risk, or diversifiable risk or non-system risk.

Total Risk

Total risk is the total variability in the return on the asset or portfolio. The total risk is the uncertainty or volatility in return due to both security-specific and economy wide factors.

Country Risk

Country risks means investment risks within the country is known as country risk. The uncertain or changes of return in respect of an investment in a foreign country is known as country risk.

FUNDAMENTAL ANALYSIS IN INVESTMENT MANAGEMENT

Fundamental analysis refers to an examination of the intrinsic worth of the company. This is done by studying the various aspects of the company in terms of the background and performance of the industry at which the belongs and the general economic and socio-political scenario of the country. However, the fundamental analysis of the investment management involves three major steps. They are as outlined below that:

- Economic Analysis
- Industry Analysis
- Company Analysis

Economic Analysis

Economic factors play a crucial role in any investment decisions that is made for taking a gain and better return to investor. Economic analysis and company performance forecasting is necessary for making investment management.

If any decision is so risk, it can be very difficult to implement in the investment by the investor. Economic analysis involved in micro level and macro level of the company's performance. Micro economics is refers to study in a small problems of the investment company. In another sense, the macro economics refers to study of overall problems of the investment company.

Economic Factors Influenced to Investment Management

Exhibit 6.1 Economic Factors influenced to Investment Management

- Demand of security from the investor. It has created a heavy demand for security. If demand, the price value of the securities is increased in the market.
- Demand and supply is also influenced to investment in terms of supply of securities is greater, the result is the price of securities is reduced.
- If demand for security, there is no supply, in this circumstance, the price of such companies shares is high.
- Economic factors has help to creation of savings.
- Economy tells something about how to effective way to earn income and then how to convert a successful saving avenues to the common people.
- Economical factors are favour with investment decisions. If inflation, the result is price increased for commodities. At the same time, business earn more profit that will convert as saving. If deflation the commodities price is reduced. At the same time, common people save money and then will investment companies.

Population: Population is the important study aspects for economist. In the case of population growth, its created huge investment opportunities, avenues to the investor. Therefore, the vast population is the expected high demand for commodities. This result is a new source of investment formation by the investor. If the population is slowdown, that final effect is investment activities and opportunities reduced because of slowdown of population growth. Consequently, investment activities are not growth.

Government spent funds for establishment of Research and Technological Development. Investor largely invest in funds and shares.

It is growth for investment activity. This result is growth of industries in the country.

Investment avenues are generated savings. Small savings made by individual investors are ready to invest in company shares, debenture and securities in terms of investor created huge capital formation.

Discovery of natural resource which is brings development and growth of investment management. Effective utilisation of raw materials that needed investments. Developed countries are invested unnatural resource products and earning yield from their investment. And discovery of energy power influence to technology. Technology is focus on lot of changes in investment area.

Forecasting

Investor should make an economic forecasting for taking a decision on securities and financial market. Forecasting is an important to forecast economic environment. Therefore, in the case of investor purchases or selling of the securities in the market at the right time. They can expect high yield from their investment. If economic conditions are fluctuated at the time the investor to take care for investment avenues. When economic conditions are favourable that benefited to the investor. They are expected good return from the investment. The company's profit depends on the factors of production such as land, labour, capital, technology, finance, government and political climate.

Economic Indicators

Economic indicators are helpful to determine the future course of action. An important economic indicators in terms of fiscal policy, monetary policy, GDP, stock prices, financial market. These factors influence to investor for investment activity.

- Rise in saving
- Create employment opportunities
- High interest rate

Above are the positive indications of the economy.

Economic Forecasting

India has a mixed economy, where the public sector plays a vital role. It means, the government being the biggest investor and spender. Investor forecasting economic trends such economic and political stability in the form of stable and long term economic policies. Its result is heavy investment in the economy. Political uncertainty and adverse changes in government policy do adversely affect industrial growth. This effect is that the investor are not investing projects.

At any stage in the economy, there are some industries that are growing while other industries are declining.

Different Phases of Economy

There are difficult phases of economy. They are as outlined below:

- Boom
- Depression
- Recession

The Indian economy depends basically on the monsoon and the growth rate of agriculture.

ECONOMIC FORECASTING TECHNIQUES

Economic Forecasting Techniques are as notified below:

- Surveys
- Economic Indicators
- Diffusion Indexes
- Economic Modeling
- Opportunistic Model Building

Surveys

Survey means personal contact of the respondent to obtain information about the price of the share, investment trends, performance and efficiency of the organisations. This type of forecasting help to research. Research to conduct empirical studies with regarding to economic conditions and its impact on stock exchange.

Economic Indicators

Economic indicators indicated that economy process in the country. This method is planned to get indications in future selecting to business growth and prosperity. Economic indicators help to investor to different phases of economy like boom, depression and rescission.

Diffusion Indexes

Diffusion indexes is also known as a census or a composite index. It is identified the weakness and strength of a specific time serious of data.

In this techniques both micro and macro economic tools are combined. This method is a extremely difficult to draw out a proper understanding of the forecasting methods.

Economic Model Building

Economic model building is a mathematical and statistical application to forecast the future trend of the economy. This technique used only by those are trained and it is used to draw out conclusions between two or more variables. This process technique specifies a particular system and calculates the results from two variables.

Opportunistic Model Building

It is also called as sectoral analysis of the gross national product model building. This method uses the national accounting data to be able to forecast for a future short term period. This method should be added to gross domestic investment, government purchases of goods in services, consumption expenses and net exports.

INDUSTRY ANALYSIS

Meaning of Industry

Industry refers to manufacturing activity concerned with the conversion of raw materials or semifinished goods into finished goods. In another meaning, it refers to that branch of business activity which is concerned with the raising, production, processing or fabrication of products.

Types of Industries

Industries or Industrial activities can be further classified into four categories. They are as mentioned below:

- Extractive Industries
- Genetic Industries
- Construction Industries
- Manufacturing Industries

Extractive Industries

Extractive industries refer to those activities which are concerned with the extraction or production of wealth from soil, air, water or from beneath the surface of the earth. They include as:

- Agriculture
- Mining

- Fishing
- Lumbering
- Hunting
- Fruit gathering

Genetic Industries

Genetic industries refer to those activities which are undertaken for reproducing or multiplying plants and animals with the object of earning profit from their sale.

Examples are:

- Nurseries raising seedlings and plants
- Cattle breeding
- Poultry farming etc.

Construction Industries

Construction industries refer to those activities which are concerned with the creation of infrastructure necessary for economic development.

Examples are:

- Construction of buildings, roads, bridges, lines, dams, canals etc.

Manufacturing Industries

Manufacturing industries refer to activities with the creation of form utility. It means that, raw material converted into finished goods.

Examples are:

- Conversion of raw cotton into cotton textiles.
- Conversion of raw jute into jute manufactures.
- Production of sugar from sugarcane.
- Production of iron and steel from iron ore etc.

Types of Manufacturing Industry

Manufacturing industries may be sub-divided into four types. They are:

- Analytical Industries
- Synthetic Industries
- Processing Industries
- Assembly Line Industries

Analytical industries

Analytical industries refers to those manufacturing industries which produce many types of products by analysing and separating the same basic raw materials into different products.

For example:

Oil refining is an analytical industry. In oil refining, the same crude oil is analysed and separated into different products like petrol, diesel oil, kerosene, lubricating oil etc.

Synthetic industries

Synthetic industries refer to all those manufacturing industries where various materials are combined together in the manufacturing process to manufacture a new product.

For example:

- Cement industry is a synthetic industry.

i.e., cement is produced by a cement industry by combining many materials like as concrete, gypsum, coal etc.

Processing industries

Processing industries refer to those manufacturing industries where the raw materials are processed through different stages/process into finished goods.

For example:

- Textile Industry
- Paper Industry

Assembly line industries

Assembly line industries refer to those manufacturing industries where different component parts already manufactured are assembled into final products.

For example:

- Automobile Industry
- Television Industry

INDUSTRY LIFE CYCLE

Industry should analyse and interpret through its life cycle.

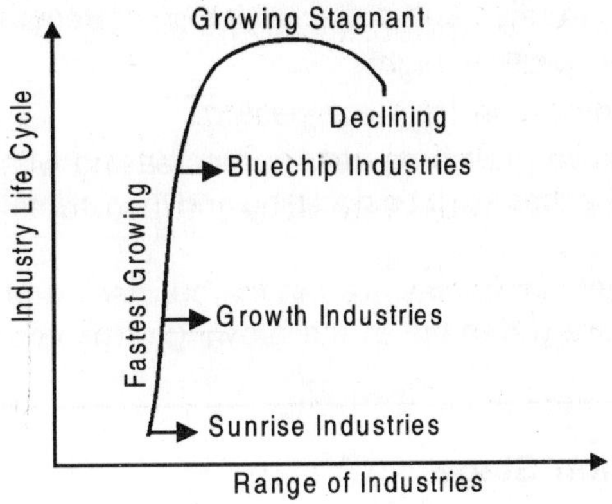

Fig. 6.1 Industry Life Cycle

Figure 6.1 has shows the relationship between the cycle of growth and range of industries.

Different cycles of growth process/stages are outlined below:

- Fastest growing companies
- Growing companies
- Stagnant companies
- Declining stages of the companies

Different range of industries are:

- Sunrise Industries
- Growth Oriented Industries
- Blue Chip Companies

This figure 6.1 clearly notified that if industry is prosperous, the companies within the industries may also be growth, if the economy is also doing well.

Fastest Growing Companies/The Pioneering Stage

According to fastest growing companies/the pioneering stage, when the new inventions and technological developments take place.

Exhibit 6.2 Features of Fastest Growing/Pioneering Companies

- In this stage, Active Investor will notice a great increased in the activity of the company.
- Production can raise and there will be great demand for the product.
- In this stage, profit is high.
- A heavy competition from competitors.
- The competitive pressures keep on increasing with the entry of new firms and the prices keep on declining and then ultimately the companies profits fall.
- A few efficient companies are run the business and most of the other companies are wiped out in the growing or pioneering stages of the companies.

Growing/Expansion Stage

Exhibit 6.3 Features of Growing/Expansion Stage

- In this stage, further investment is needed.
- Product and services price is stabilised.
- Companies are earn huge profits.
- Investor yield on good return from investment.
- Companies are internally generated funds to keep financial requirement of the organisation.
- This stages also known as maturity stages for companies.
- Companies are started expansion and diversification of products.
- During this stage, companies introducing different variety of products.

Stagnant Industries/Stagnant Stage

Exhibit 6.4 Features of Stagnant Industries

- Increase in sales.
- Profits of the company is some extent to reduced.
- During this stage, growth is also reduced.
- Company has spent huge amount for advertisement for promotion of goods and service.
- Investors are plan and careful about their investment avenues in the business.
- Investors cautious about future plan and ready to sell their securities in the financial market.

Declining Stages of Industries

Exhibit 6.5 Features of Declining Stages of Industries

- Companies are continuously making loss in the business.
- Investor has not received yield in terms of dividend.
- Customers are rejected to declining companies product.
- Even investors are lost their principal amount.
- Expenditure is increased and revenues is decreased.
- Companies are closed their business units.
- Investor looks for new investment opportunities.

INDUSTRY GROUPS

Industry groups can be classified:

- On the basis of normal sizewise classification
- On the basis of proprietory based classification
- On the basis of use based classification
- On the basis of input based classification

On the Basis of Normal Sizewise Classification

It can be further classified into as follows:

- Small scale units
- Medium scale units
- Large sized industries

On the Basis of Proprietory Based Classification

Industries have been classified on the basis of proprietary.

- Private Sector Industries
- Public Sector Industries
- Joint Sector (Jointly owned by private and public) Industries.

On the Basis of Use Based Classification

Industries have also been classified on the basis of use based.

- Basic Industries
- Capital Goods Industries
- Intermediate Goods
- Consumer Goods Industries

On the Basis of Input Based Classification

- Agro based products
- Forest based products
- Marine based products
- Metal based products
- Chemical based products

SOURCES OF INFORMATION FOR ANALYSIS

Exhibit 6.6 Sources of Information for Analysis

An important sources of information for industry analysis as outlined below that:

- RBI Reports on currency and finance bulletin.
- Monthly bulletin of RBI on industrial production, prices etc.
- Data on industries which are published by the Ministry of Industry and Commerce.
- Many Industry Associations has been published data.
- FICCI and Associations shall also publish Industry data.
- RBI data relating to industries.

Key Factors to be Examined for Sources of Data

Exhibit 6.7 Key Factors to be Examined for Sources of Data

Major key factors are:

- Looks for past, present and future trends of the industry
- Analyse the past sales and earning performance of the industry
- To know the stage of growth of the industry
- Government rules and regulation towards the industry
- To know the present labour conditions
- To analyse the competitive conditions and industry share prices in market
- To analyse industry life cycle and its effect.

Influencing Factors of Industry Analysis

Influencing factors of Industry Analysis as mentioned below:

- Product line
- Raw material and output

- Capacity installed and utilised
- Industry characteristic
- Demand and market
- Government policy with regard to industry
- Labour and other industrial problems
- Management
- Future prospects

Product Line

Product line refers to in terms of the product life cycle like introduction, growth, maturity, saturation and decline stages of the product. Product line influenced to industry. Therefore, industry depends on product or service which is offered by company.

Raw Materials

Industry refers to raw material convert into finished goods/products. Companies always look for raw material from different suppliers and select supplier who is supplying raw material at less and competitive price. When raw materials are scarce, this time, companies are ready to pay more price to suppliers and get raw materials. Some times companies are importing same materials and pay more price. Those things are directly influenced to profit the companies.

Capacity Installed and Utilised

Industrial products demand estimating by the Planning Commission and Government. Whenever industry is utilised full installed capacity, it will earn huge profit and even produced goods at low manufacturing cost. If under utilisation of plant, therefore, the product price is increased. Industry will estimate future demand and how to meet future requirements then they are installed full capacity of the plant and machinery.

Industry Characteristics

Industry characteristics are:

- Cyclical Industry
- Fluctuate Industry
- Stability Industry
- Decline Industry

Demand and Market

High demand from customer that creates increased the price of the product if supply of the product is less. Low demand which creates decreased the price of the product, if the supply product is more. In market, a heavy competition to sell identical goods. It's result is very less profit, therefore, competition created similar industries the market.

Government Policy with Regard to Industry

- Industrial policies
- Government rules and regulations
- Licence
- Granting of clearances
- Reservation for small scale industry products

Labour and Other Industrial Problems

Whether industry either capital or labour intensive has to utilise labour effectively and efficiently. Power, Infrastructure, Labour, Transportation, Communication, Raw materials, Finance and poor productivity problems are Industry.

Management

If Industry well planned, organised, monitored and controlled in a complex and difficult situations, management are efficient and capable to face and run into successful way of industry. The management has appraised in terms of their capabilities, popularity, honesty and integrity.

Future Prospectus

Future prospectus such as:

- Capacity utilisation
- Demand and markets
- Government policy
- Availability of inputs
- Infrastructure etc.

Future prospectus means to study of overall these problems and prospectus of Industry.

Above factors are helpful to industry analysis and interpretations of past, present and future trends of the industry.

COMPANY ANALYSIS

Company analysis is a study of the variables which influence the future of a company both qualitatively and quantitatively.

Qualitative Factors

Exhibit 6.8 Qualitative Factors

Qulitative factors are as identified below:

- Management efficiency
- Rating of promoters
- Rating of collaborators
- Uniqueness of the product
- Location of government policy and patronage etc.

Management Efficiency

Management efficiency is the most important variable influencing the company's performance, management efficiency namely in terms of:

- The quality of the product
- Capability of the administration
- Popularity of the company image
- Close integrity of the management

Rating of Promoters

Rating of promoters and management looks for:

- Their planning
- Financial management of the company
- Growth orientation programme of the company
- Company's expansion plans
- Effective tax planning management
- A well equipped R&D and technology of the company
- The company popularity is known from track record, retention policy, distribution of yield (Dividend) and bonus and liquidity position.

Rating of Collaborators

A company collaboration of foreign companies and Indian companies. Collaboration stands for accomplishment of long term objectives of the companies. Collaboration is the agreement between one company to another company. Both companies are necessary to cooperate for accomplishing the short and long term benefits from each other.

Uniqueness of the Product

Company data are to be examined from the point of view of the installed capacity and its utilisation of raw materials, components, processing, cost production, profit margins, demand and supply. These factors are analyse the uniqueness of the product.

Location of Government Policy and Patronage etc.

Government policy like Industrial Policy and special privileges for small scale industry and large scale industries. Now a days, Government encourages to companies to start industrialisation and also patronage in terms of incentives, subsidies, is given to companies for growth of the economy.

Quantitative Factors

Quantitative factors are as identified below:

- Capital efficiency
- Sales Turnover
- Profitability margins

Quantitative factors are important from the point of view of company analysis, quantitative factors are highlights of the financial position of the companies. These factors are influenced by the industry and economy, quantitative factors are influenced to the capacity utilisation, demand, cost and margins. The fundamentals of the company are to be analysed in terms of its financial structure, leverage, liquidity and profitability and financial viability etc. For this purpose, the information is to be secured from the annual reports of the company, balance sheets, press reports, AGMs reports, management's press releases and publications of the industry and commerce associations.

FINANCIAL STATEMENT ANALYSIS

Financial statements are an important source of information for evaluating the performance and growth of a firm. In the case of properly analysed and interpreted to financial statements which can provide valuable insights into a firm's performance. Analysis of financial interest is to interest of short term and long term investors, security analysts, managers, government, financial institution and others. Financial statement analysis in terms of variety of purposes to assess short term and long term liquidity position of the firm to detail assessment of the strengths and weakness of the farm in various areas. It is helpful to assess corporate excellence, judging, creditworthiness, forecasting bond ratings, evaluating intrinsic value of equity shares, predicting bankruptcy and assessing market risk.

An Accountant prepares two principal statements as outlined below:

- The Balance Sheet
- The Profit and Loss Account

In additionally, an accountant prepares an ancillary statement like as:

- Cash flow statement

Balance Sheet

The balance sheet shows the financial position of a business at a given specific point of time. As per the Companies Act, the balance sheet of a company shall be either the account horizontal form or the report (vertical) form. Exhibit 6.9 shows that these forms; Part A of this exhibit the account Form and Part B the report Form.

Exhibit 6.9 Balance Sheet Structure

A. Account Form

Liabilities	***Assets***
• Share Capital	• Fixed assets
• Reserves and Surplus	• Investments
• Secured Loans	• Current assets, loans and advances
• Current liabilities and provisions	• Current assets
• Current liabilities	• Loans and advances
• Provisions	• Miscellaneous expenditure and losses

B. Report Form

I. Sources of Funds
   (1) Shareholder's Funds
      (a) Share capital
      (b) Reserve and Surplus
   (2) Loan Funds
      (a) Secured Loans
      (b) Unsecured Loans

II. Application of Funds
   (1) Fixed Asset
   (2) Investments
   (3) Current assets, loans and advances
      Less: Current liabilities and provisions
      Net: Current assets
   (4) Miscellaneous expenditure and losses

Liabilities

Liabilities defined very broadly refers to the amount due by the business to others. The Companies Act classifies as:

- Share capital
- Reserve and Surplus
- Secured loans
- Unsecured loans
- Current liabilities and provisions

Share Capital

Share capital is further divided into two types:

- Equity capital
- Preference capital

Equity capital represents the contribution of equity shareholders who are the real owners of the company. Equity capital is being risk capital. It carries no fixed rate of dividend.

Preference capital represents the contribution of preference shareholders and it carries fixed rate of dividend.

Reserves and Surplus

Reserves and surplus are profits which have been retained in company. There are two types of reserves. They are as below:

- Revenue reserves
- Capital reserves

Revenue reserves represent accumulated retained earnings from the profits of normal business operations. Different types of revenue reserves are:

- General reserve
- Investment allowance reserve
- Capital redemption reserves
- Dividend equilisation reserves etc.

Capital reserves arise out of gains which are not related to normal business operations. For instance of such gains are the premium on issue of shares or farm on revaluation of assets.

Surplus is the balance in the profit and loss account that has not been appropriated to any particular reserve account.

Secured Loans

Secured loans are the borrowings of the company against which specific collateral have been provided. The secured loans consists of important components are as below:

- Debentures
- Loans from financial institutions
- Loans from commercial banks

Unsecured Loans

Unsecured loans the borrowings of the company which no specific security has been provided. The important components of unsecured loans are as below:

- Fixed deposits
- Loan and advances from promoters
- Inter corporate borrowings
- Unsecured loans from banks

Current Liabilities and Provision

It consists of the amounts which due to the suppliers of goods and services bought on credit, advance payment received, outstanding/accrued expenses, unclaimed dividend, provision for taxes, dividends etc.

Current liabilities are those liabilities which are expected to mature in the next twelve months. i.e., which are repayable within one year from the date of the balance sheet.

Assets

Assets represents property, things or resources owned by the company. Assets are some value to the company. Assets have been acquired at a specific monetary cost by the firm for conduct of its operations. According to Companies Act, assets classified as below:

- Fixed Assets
- Investments
- Current Assets
- Miscellaneous expenditure and loss

Fixed Assets

Fixed assets are those assets which are acquired for use over very long periods for carrying on the operations of the firm and they are not meant for resale. Fixed Assets are:

- Land
- Buildings
- Plant
- Machinery
- Patents
- Copy rights

Investments

Investment means financial securities owned by the company. Some investments represent long term commitment of funds like equity shares. And others investments are to be short term in nature like as mutual fund schemes.

Current Assets, Loans and Advances

Current assets, loans and advances consists of cash and other assets that get converted into cash during the operating cycle of the company. Current assets are those assets which are convert into cash within a year. The current assets consists of as below:

- Cash
- Sundry debtors
- Inventories
- Loans and advances
- Prepaid expenses

Miscellaneous Expenditures and Losses

It consists of two items. They are:

- Miscellaneous expenditures
- Loss

Miscellaneous expenditures represent certain outlays like preliminary expenses and development expenses that have not been written off.

A loss represents a decrease in owners' equity.

Profit and Loss Account

The Companies Act has prescribed a standard format for the balance sheet, but not for the profit and loss account. The companies act has also specified that the profit and loss account should show specific information as required by Schedule IV.

The profit and loss account may be presented in the account form or report form. The report form statement may be a single-step statement or a multistep statement. Under single step statement, first record all revenue items, then the expense items are shown and finally given the net profit of the company.

Exhibit 6.10 Single Step form of Profit and Loss Acount

Income	
Sales	xxx
Expenditure	
Material and other expenditure	xxx
Interest	xxx
Depreciation	xxx
Profit before tax	xxx
Provision for tax	xxx
Profit after tax	xxx
Profit period adjustments	xxx
Profit available for appropriations	xxx
Appropriations	
Debenture redemption reserve	xxx
Dividend	xxx
General reserve	xxx
Surplus carried to balance sheet	xxx

Exhibit 6.10 provides total of revenues and expenses. Multistep profit and loss account provides separated information. In additionally, it shown final profit measures.

Exhibit 6.11 Multi-step form of Profit and Loss Account

Net Sales	xxx	
Cost of Goods sold		
Stocks	xxx	
Wages and Salaries	xxx	
Other manufacturing expenses	xxx	xxx
Gross profit		xxx
Operating Expenses		
Depreciation	xxx	
General administration	xxx	
Selling expenses	xxx	xxx
Operating profit		xxx
Non-operating surplus/deficit		
Profit before interest and tax		xxx
Interest	xxx	

Tax before tax		xxx
Tax	xxx	
Profit after tax	xxx	
Dividends	xxx	
Retained earnings		xxx
Per share data		xxx
Earning per share		xxx
Dividend per share		xxx
Market price per share		xxx
Book value per share		

Cash Flow Statement

Cash flow statement means how company generates cash and spends cash. It generates cash when it issues securities, raises a bank loan, sells a product and sale of an assets. It spends cash when it repays loans, pay interest, dividends, purchases materials, acquires an asset etc. The generally activities that generate cash are called sources of cash and the generally activities that absorb cash are called uses of cash.

FINANCIAL RATIOS

Ratio means: A ratio is an arithmetical relationship between two figures. Financial ratios may be classified as follows:

- Liquidity ratios
- Leverage ratios
- Turnover ratios
- Profitability ratios
- Valuation ratios

Liquidity Ratios

Liquidity refers to the ability of a company to meet its obligations in the short run, usually a year. Liquidity ratios are typically based on the relationship between current assets and current liabilities. The important liquidity ratios are:

- Current ratio
- Acid test ratio
- Cash ratio

Current Ratio

Current ratio also called as working capital ratio. It establishes the relationship between total current assets and current liabilities. Current ratio is a very popular ratio, it can be defined as:

$$\frac{\text{Current Assets}}{\text{Current Liabilities}}$$

The major components of current assets

- Cash in Hand
- Cash at Bank
- Bills Receivable
- Sundry Debtors
- Stock of raw materials, work in progress and finished goods
- Short term Investments
- Prepaid Expenses
- Accrued Income

The major components of current liabilities

- Sundry Creditors
- Bills Payable
- Bank Overdraft
- Outstanding Expenses
- Income received in Advance
- Provision for Taxation
- Short Term Borrowings
- Unclaimed Dividend
- Proposed Dividend

The standard norm of current ratio is 2:1.

Acid Test Ratio

Acid test ratio concerned with the relationship between liquid assets and liquid liabilities. It is also called the quick ratio or liquid ratios. The acid test ratio is defined as:

$$\frac{\text{Quick Assets}}{\text{Current Assets}}$$

Quick assets are defined as current assets excluding inventories and prepaid expenses.

The standard norm of Acid Test Ratio is 1:1. It is based on those current assets which are highly liquid.

Cash Ratio/Absolute Liquid Ratio

This ratio establishes a relationship between absolute liquid assets to quick liabilities. Cash ratio defined as

$$\text{Cash Ratio} = \frac{\text{Cash and Bank Balance} + \text{Current Investments}}{\text{Current Liabilities}}$$

Leverage Ratios

Financial leverage means to the use of debt finance. Debt capital is the cheaper source of finance. It is also a riskier source of finance. Leverage ratios generally helpful in assessing the risk arising from the use of debt capital. Financial leverage commonly analysed by two types of ratios are

- Structural Ratios
- Coverage Ratios

Structural ratios are based on the proportions of debt and equity in the financial structure of the company. An important structural ratios are:

- Debt equity ratio
- Debt asset ratio

Coverage ratios show the relationship between debt servicing commitments and sources for meeting these burdens. An important coverage ratio are:

- Interest coverage ratio
- Fixed charges ratio
- Debt service coverage ratio

Debt Equity Ratios

Debt equity ratio expresses the relationship between debt and equity. Debt equity ratio is defined as

$$\frac{\text{Debt}}{\text{Equity}} \text{ or } \frac{\text{External equities}}{\text{Internal equities}}$$

Debt consist of short term as well as long term debt equity consist of net worth plus preference capital.

Debt Asset Ratio

Debt assets ratio shows the relationship between the debt and asset. It is defined as:

$$\frac{\text{Debt}}{\text{Assets}}$$

Debt consists of short term as well as long term debt. Assets consists of the total of all assets.

Interest Coverage Ratio

Interest coverage ratio shows the relationship between profit before interest and taxes and interest. Interest coverage ratio is defined as:

$$\frac{\text{Profit before Interest and Taxes}}{\text{Interest}}$$

A high interest coverage ratio refers that the firm can easily meet its interest burden even if earnings before interest and taxes suffer a considerable decline.

A low interest coverage ratio may result in financial embarrassment when earning before interest and taxes decline.

Fixed Charges Coverage Ratio

This ratio shows the relationship between profit before interest and taxes plus depreciation and debt interest and taxes covers all fixed financing charges. This ratio is defined as:

$$\frac{\text{Profit before Interest and Taxes} + \text{Depreciation}}{\text{Interest} + (\text{Repayment of loan} / 1 \square \text{Tax rate})}$$

Debt Service Coverage Ratio

This ratio is defined as:

$$\frac{\text{Profit after tex} + \text{Depreciation} + \text{Other non cash charges} + \text{Interest on term loan}}{\text{Interest on term loan} + \text{Repayment of term loan}}$$

Turn Over Ratios/Activity Ratios/Performance Ratio

Turn over ratios indicate the performance of an organisation. These ratios are based on the relationship between the level of activity in terms of sales or cost of goods sold and levels of various assets. An important ratios are:

- Stock/inventory turnover ratio
- Average collection period
- Receivables/Debtor turnover ratio
- Fixed assets turnover
- Total assets turnover

Stock/Inventory Turnover Ratio

This ratio establishes the relationship between the cost of goods sold during a given period and average stock holding during that period.

It measures how fast the stock is moving through the company and generating sales. It is defined as

$$\frac{\text{Cost of goods sold}}{\text{Average inventory}}$$

This ratio reflects the efficiency of inventory management.

Debtor Turnover Ratio

This ratio explains the relationship of net credit sales of a company to its book debts indicating at the rate at which cash is generated by turnover of receivables or debtors. This is defined as:

$$\frac{\text{Net credit sales}}{\text{Avereage sundry debtors}}$$

Average Debtors = Opening Debtors + Opening Bills Receivable + Closing Debtors + Closing Bills Receivables/2.

Average Collection Period

It represents the number of days worth of credit sales which is locked in Sundry debtors. This is defined as:

$$\frac{\text{Average debtors}}{\text{Average daily credit sales}}$$

or

$$\text{Average Collection Period} = \frac{365}{\text{Debtors turnover}}$$

Fixed Assets Turnover

It shows the relationship between the net sales and average net fixed assets. This is defined as:

$$\frac{\text{Net sales}}{\text{Average net fixed assets}}$$

Total Assets Turnover

It shows the relationship between the net sales and average total assets. It is defined as:

$$\frac{\text{Net sales}}{\text{Average total assets}}$$

Profitability Ratios

It reflects the final result of business operations. There are two types of profitability ratios.

- Profit margin ratios
- Rate of return ratios

Profit margin ratios shows the relationship between profit and sales. Gross profit ratio and net profit ratios are the examples of profit margin ratios.

Gross profit ratio: It is defined as:

$$\frac{\text{Gross profit}}{\text{Net sales}}$$

Net Profit Ratio

Net profit ratio is defined as:

$$\frac{\text{Net profit}}{\text{Net sales}}$$

Return on Total Assets

This ratio is defined as:

$$\frac{\text{Net income (p rofit)}}{\text{Average total assets}}$$

It is also called as return on capital employed/return on investment.

Earning Power Ratio

It is defined as:

$$\frac{\text{Equity earning}}{\text{Average equity}}$$

Valuation Ratios

It indicate how the equity stock of the company is assessed in the capital market. It reflects the combined induced of risk and return, it measures of a company's performance. An important valuation ratios are:

- Price earning ratio
- Yield
- Market value to book value ratio

Price Earning Ratio

It is defined as:

$$\frac{\text{Market price per share}}{\text{Earning per share}}$$

Yield

It is defined as:

$$\frac{\text{Dividend + price change}}{\text{Initial price}}$$

Market Value to Book Value Ratio

This ratio is defined as:

$$\frac{\text{Market value per share}}{\text{Book value per share}}$$

COST BENEFITS ANALYSIS

In making investments in financial assets like deposits, bonds, debentures, shares etc. It involves investment management. Investment management involves a cost benefit analysis.

The cost involved the risk. And benefits involved the returns.

Risk arises due to non-payment of dividend, interest, delay or non-payment of principal, variability of return or market value of investments. Risk may be classified as:

- Company risk
- Market risk
- Business risk
- Commodity/Product risk
- Financial risk
- Economy risk of the Nation
- International factors

Risk is also influenced by external and internal considerations. Internal risk considerations are controllable and external risks are uncontrollable and it broadly affect investments. External risks are known as systematic risk. Internal risks are known as unsystematic risk.

CLASSIFICATION OF RISKS

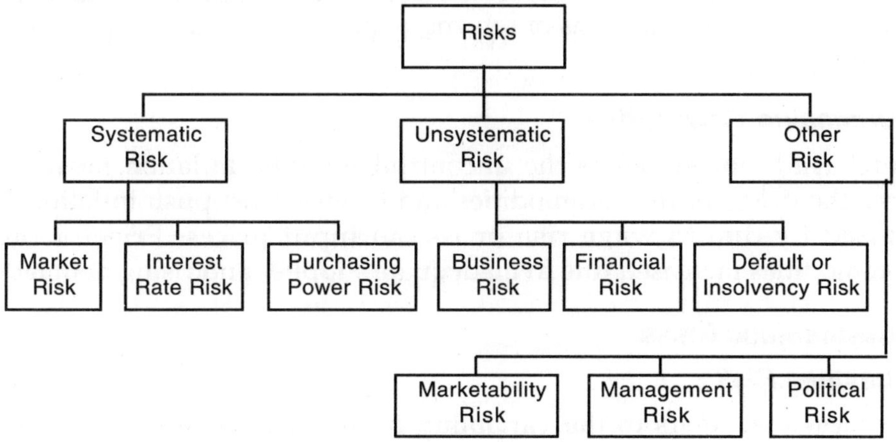

Fig. 6.2 Classification of Risks

Figure 6.2 has indicates the classification of risks. Risks may be classified as:

- Systematic risk
- Unsystematic risk
- Other risk

Systematic risks are market risk, interest rate risk and purchasing power risk.

Unsystematic risks are business risk, financial risk and default or insolvency risk.

Other risks are marketability risks, management risks and political risks.

Systematic Risks

Market Risk

Market risk arises out of changes in Demand and Supply of goods and service in the markets. Market risk is unpredictable. It is not controllable. It is uncontrollable factors of the risk. Investors have failure due to lack of knowledge of market.

Interest Rate Risk

Investment always expected to return in terms of interest rate. Interest rate changes from time to time. The loan borrowed by companies and stock brokers generally depend on interest rates. When interest rate is changed, while the market activity and investor perceptions change with the changes in interest rates. The monetary and fiscal policy that is not controllable by the investor affects the riskness of investment due to their effects in terms of returns, expectations and total principal amount.

Purchasing Power Risk

Purchasing power risk is the uncontrollable risk. Inflation means it rises the prices of the commodities and service. Cost push inflation is caused by due to wage rise or rise in input prices. Price of the commodities increased due to inadequate supplies and rising demand.

Unsystematic Risks

Business Risk

Business risk refers to the variability of the business, sales, income, profits etc. It can depend on the market conditions for the product mix, input supplies, strength of competitors etc. Business risk is internal risk due to fall in production, labour problems, raw material problems or inadequate supply of electricity etc. It leads to fall in revenues and in profit of the company.

Financial Risk

Financial risk refers to the method of financing, adopted by the company, high leverage leading to larger debt servicing problems or short term liquidity problems due to bad debts, delayed receivables and fall in current assets or rise in current liabilities. Financial problems in terms of earnings, profits, dividends.

Default or Insolvency Risk

The borrower/issuer of securities may become insolvent due to default or delay the payment in terms of installments or principal repayments.

Other Risks

Political Risks

Political risks refers to changes in the government, tax rate, monetary policy, fiscal policy, impositions control and administrative regulations etc.

Management Risk

Management risk refers to error and inefficiencies of management, causing losses to the company.

Marketability Risks

It refers to involve loss of liquidity or loss of value in conversions from one asset to another.

Benefits Analysis

Benefits involved return in terms of regular incomes (interest and dividends), capital appreciation, safety and security of funds, marketability and liquidity of investments. The investor has to assess the costs and benefits of each investment.

ENVIRONMENTAL CONSIDERATIONS

Investor has to take into consideration the environmental factors in investment management. Investors past background, family requirements, the assets of neighbours and colleagues. In additionally, other external factors may influence his investment decisions.

Rural and semi urban areas people are influenced by their immediate environment and access to investment avenues. The agriculturist invests in ploughs, tractors and other requirements. These are needed for his occupation and environment. Beyond these, investor invest in gold, silver and real estate.

Urban and Metropolitan people are invests in vehicles, consumer durables, mutual funds, corporate securities and various other instruments.

Semi-urban and urban areas people invests in housing finance companies, finance and investment companies and chit funds.

CHIT FUNDS AND NIDHIS MANAGEMENT

Chit funds and Nidhis are mostly governed by State Acts and partly controlled by the RBI in respect of their deposit raising activities.

Chit funds may be various types:

- Prize chits
- Normal and conventional chits
- Lottery chits

They collects the savings from savers on a monthly/weekly basis and lend.

Disadvantages

(1) Chit fund promoters fly-by-night operators who collect the funds and misuse them for trading and speculation.

(2) Chit and Nidhi may not always be safe.

While investors should be careful in taking risk of investment in deposits in the chits, nidhis.

TAX PLANNING IN INVESTMENT MANAGEMENT

Tax planning means reduce the tax liability at lowest possible point of the investor. In this purpose, investor using tax exemptions, tax rebates, deductions, tax holiday's and tax benefits to their investment.

Taxation of Dividend and Interest Income

The dividend and interest incomes consisting the returns from mutual funds, bank deposits etc., used to enjoy a tax rebate. PPF, Tax free bonds, Rahit Patra are exemption from tax.

Capital Gains

Securities are holding less than 12 months as known as short term capital gain or which are chargeable under normal income tax slabs.

Securities are holding more than 12 months as known as long term capital gain, which tax rate is only 20%. For investments other than securities like gold, real asset which held for 36 months to be considered as long term capital gains.

Wealth Tax

Shares, debentures of companies, PPF, NSS, Capital Investment Bonds, National Defence Bonds, Postal Deposits etc., are all exempted from wealth tax. But other assets like gold, jewelry, house and real estate etc. are subject to wealth tax.

QUESTIONS FOR DISCUSSIONS

1. Define the following:
    - Default risk
    - Financial risk
    - Liquidity risk

- Maturity risk
- Call risk
- Interested rate risk
- Inflation risk
- Exchange risk
- Country risk
- Systematic risk
- Unsystematic risk
- Surveys
- Economic indicators

2. What is investment management?
3. Explain the risk under investment management.
4. What are the procedure and criteria for investment decisions?
5. Described the fundamental analysis in investment management.
6. Explain the economic analysis. What are the economic factors influenced to investment management?
7. Discuss the economic forecasting techniques.
8. Discuss the industry and its types.
9. Describe the industry life cycle.
10. Explain the sources of information for analysis.
11. Explain the company analysis.
12. Briefly discuss about the financial statements.
13. Explain the financial ratios.
14. Explain the liquidity ratio.
15. Explain the leverage ratio.
16. Explain the turnover ratios.
17. Explain the profitability ratios.
18. Explain the valuation ratios.
19. Discuss the cost benefit analysis.
20. What is environmental consideration?
21. Discuss the chit funds and nidhis management.
22. Explain the tax planning in investment management.

REFERENCES

Amling, Investment, *An introduction to Analysis and Management,* Prentice Hall, Englewood Cliffs, New Jersey, U.S.A, 1984.

Fischer and Jordon, *Security Analysis and Portfolio Management,* Prentice Hall, Englewood Clifs, New Jersey, USA, 1983.

Fred Bennick, *Introduction to Investments and Finance: Theory and Analysis,* MacMillan, New York, 1971.

Hayes and Hauman, *Investment Analysis and Management,* McGraw Hill, USA, 1976.

Steven Botten, *Security Analysis and Portfolio Management: An Analytical Investment,* Holt Rinehart and Winson IWC, New York, 1972.

Prasanna Chandra, *Investment Analysis and Portfolio Management,* Tata McGraw Hill, New Delhi 2006.

CHAPTER 7

INVESTMENT AND FINANCE DECISIONS IN CAPITAL MARKET

Learning Objectives

- Special features of capital market
- Players in the new issue market: Role of registrer and merchent bankers
- Criteria for valuation of securities, bines etc.

INTRODUCTION

This chapter has been discussed to capital market, functions, structure, players in the new issue market, merchant bankers and role, stock market intermediaries, special features of capital market and valuation of securities such as bonds, stocks and convertible securities.

Capital Market Definition

Capital market: A market where debt or equity securities are traded.

Debt Definition

Debt means a liability or obligation in the form of bonds, loan notes, or mortgages, owed to another person or persons and required to be paid by a specified date (maturity).

Equity Definition

Equity means:

- Ownership interest in a corporation in the form of common stock or preferred stock.
- It also refers to total assets minus total liabilities, in which case it is also referred to as shareholder's equity or net worth.

Security Definition

Security means:

An investment instrument, like any note, stock, treasury stock, bond, debenture, certificate of interest or participation in any profit sharing agreement or in any oil, gas, or other mineral royalty or lease, any collateral trust certificate, pre-organisation certificate or subscription, transferable share, investment contract, voting trust certificate, certificate of deposits for a security, any part, call straddle, option or privilege on any security, certificate of deposit, or group or index of securities (including any interest therein or based on the value thereof), or any put call, straddle, option, or privilege entered into on a national securities exchange relating to foreign currency, or in general, any instrument commonly known is a security.

Functions of Capital Market

Exhibit 7.1 Functions of Capital Market

- Policy matters relating to the development and regulation of securities markets and investor protection
- Policy matters relating to domestic mutual funds, venture capital funds, collective investment schemes etc.
- Organisational matters relating to SEBI and Securities Appellate Tribunal (SAT)
- Policy formulation and approval of External Commercial Borrowings
- Matters relating to Unit Trust of India
- Pension Reforms
- It's responsibility of formulation of suitable policies for the development of capital market in consultation with SEBI, RBI and other agencies
- Capital market deals with all organisational matters relating to raise funds
- The capital market works as an important sources for the productive use of the economy's savings
- It provides incentives to save and facilitates capital formation by offering suitable rates of interest in terms of the price of capital
- It should provides an avenue for investors, especially for the Household Sector to invest in financial asset that are more productive than physical assets
- It facilitates increase in production and productivity in the economy. Therefore, it enhances the economic welfare of the society
- In capital market, the different financial institution operations to influence economic growth
- A good capital market principally consist of expert intermediaries promotes stability in values of securities representing capital funds.

CAPITAL MARKET

The capital market is a market for buying and selling of equity, debt and securities. Generally, it deals with long term securities that have a maturity period of above one year. Capital market may be classified into three parts:

- Industrial Securities Market
- Government Securities Market
- Long-term Loans Market

Capital Market Structure

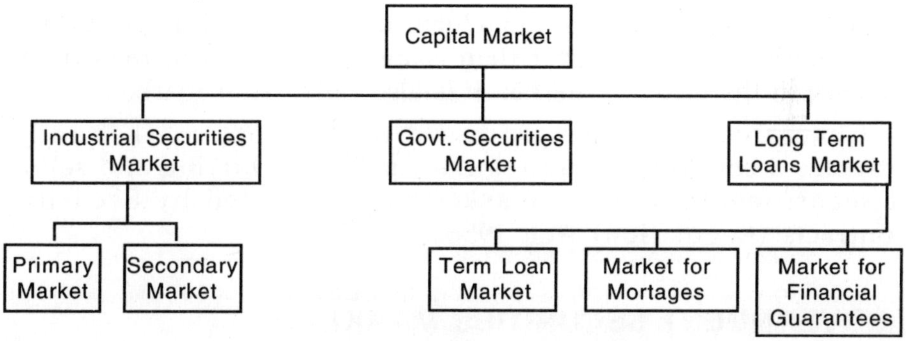

Fig. 7.1 Capital Market Structure

Figure 7.1 indicates that the capital structure. Capital market consists of the following:

- Industrial Securities Market
- Government Securities Market
- Long-term Loans Market

INDUSTRIAL SECURITIES MARKET

Industrial Securities Market includes industrial securities. They are as mentioned below:

- Equity shares or Ordinary shares
- Preference shares
- Debentures or bonds

Industrial securities market further classified into two types. They are as notified below:

- Primary Market or New Issue Market
- Secondary Market or Stock Exchange

Primary/New Issue Market

Primary market is the market for new securities issues, in the primary market the security is purchased directly from the issuer. This differs from the secondary market. The primary market facilitates capital formation.

A company may raise capital by through primary market. There are three routes to raise capital from the public.

- Public Issue
- Rights Issue
- Private Placement

Secondary Market

Secondary market is a market in which an investor purchases a security from another investor rather than issuer, subsequent to the original issuance in the primary market. It is also called after market.

Generally, securities are listed in the stock market and it provides a continuous and regular market for buying and selling of securities. Secondary market has controlled by Securities Contracts (Regulation) Act, 1956.

GOVERNMENT SECURITIES MARKET

Government securities market is also called as Gilt-Edged Securities. There are many types of Government Securities that consist of short-term and long-term Government Securities are issued by the Central Government, State Governments, Semi-Government Authorities. Government Securities are promissory notes, bearer bonds which can be discounted and Treasury bills.

LONG-TERM LOANS MARKET

Under this market, Development Banks and Commercial Banks can play a significant role. Because they are supplying long-term loans to corporate customers. Long-term loans may be classified into three types. They are as outlined below:

- Term Loans Market
- Mortgages Market
- Financial Guarantees Market

NEW ISSUE MARKET FUNCTIONS

The main and important function of the New Issue Market are as mentioned below:

- Origination
- Underwriting
- Distribution

Origination

Origination refers to the work of investigation and analysis and processing of new proposals. Origination begins before an issue is actually floated in the market. There are two important notes in this function:

- Origination involves a careful study of the technical, economic, financial and legal aspects which ensure to soundness of the project. This preliminary investigation undertaken by the sponsors of the issue.
- Advisory services which go to improve the quality of capital issues and ensures its success.

The Advisory Services include:

- Type of issue refers to the kind of securities to be issued whether equity share, preference share and debenture
- Magnitude of issue
- Time of floating an issue
- Pricing of an issue-either shares are to be issued at par or at premium
- Method of issue/floatation
- An important techniques for selling of the securities

The importance of specialised services provided by New issue market function like origination. The function of origination is done by merchant bankers who may be commercial banks, Financial Institutions even include private firms. Initially this study provided investigation and soundness of judgement is done by specialised division of commercial banks, financial institutions and private firms. Although this service is highly important, the success of this issue depends to a large extent on the efficiency of the market.

Underwriting

Underwriting is an agreement whereby the underwriter promises to subscribe to a specified number of shares or debentures or a specified amount of stock offered to the public in the event of the public not subscribing it. If public is fully subscribed then there is no liability for the underwriter. If a part of share issues remain unsold, the underwriter will ready to buy the shares. Therefore, underwriting is a guarantee for the marketability of shares.

Types of Underwriter

The underwriters in India may be classified into two broad categories/ types:

- Institutional Underwriters
- Non-Institutional Underwriters

Institutional underwriters are namely IDBI, IFCI, ICICI, LIC and UTI. These are Public Financial Institutions, Non-Institutional underwriters are Brokers.

Method of Underwriting

There are three methods to make an underwriting agreement:

- Standing behind the issue
- Outright purchase
- Consortium method

Standing behind the Issue

Under this method, the underwriter will give guarantee to the sale of specified number of shares within a specified period. In the case of public do not subscribe to the specified amount of issue, the underwriter buy the remaining amount of issues.

Outright Method

Under this method, underwriter can make outright purchase of shares and resell them to the investors.

Consortium Method

This method, underwriting is jointly done by a group of underwriters. The underwriters can form syndicate for this purpose. This method is suitable for large issues.

Advantages of Underwriting

Exhibit 7.2 Advantages of Underwriting

An important advantages are:

- Underwriting removes the risk of the issued company
- The company is assured of getting minimum subscription within the stipulated time and to a statutory obligation to be fulfilled by the issuing company
- Underwriters undertakes the burden of highly specialised functions of distributing securities
- Underwriter provides expert advise with regard to timing of security issue, the pricing of issue, the size and type of securities to be issued etc.
- Reputed underwriters influences the public to buy securities

DISTRIBUTION

Distribution is the function of sale of securities to ultimate investors. Distribution service is performed by brokers and agents who maintain regular and direct contact with the ultimate customers.

METHODS OF FLOATING NEW ISSUES

The various methods of floating of securities in the new issue market are as:

- Public issues
- Offer for sale
- Placement
- Right issues

Public Issues

In this method, the issuing company directly offers to the general public/institutions at a fixed number of shares at a stated price through a document is known as prospectus. Joint Stock Company should follow this method to raise capital by through the issue of securities. The prospectus should state the following:

- Name of the company
- Address of the registered office of the company
- Existing and proposed activities of the company
- Names of Directors
- Authorised and proposed issue capital to the public
- Dates of opening issue and closing the subscription list
- Minimum subscription
- Names of brokers/underwriters/bankers/managers and registrars to the issue
- A statement by the company that it will apply to stock exchange for quotations of its shares
- Prospectus should be attached to every share application form.

Advantages of Issue through Prospectus

Exhibit 7.3 Advantages of issue through Prospectus

- It is inviting a large section of the public through advertisement
- This method is the direct method and there is no intermediaries involved in it
- Under this method, shares are allotted on the non-discriminatory basis. It helps in wide disposal of shares and to avoid concentration of wealth in few shareholders.

Demerits

Exhibit 7.4 Demerits

- This method is an expensive method. The company has spent huge amount for printing, Advertising of prospectus, bank's commission, underwriting commission, legal charges, stamp duty listing fee and registration charges
- This method is to suitable only for large issues

Offer of Sale

Offer of sale consists in outright sale of securities through the intermediary of Issue Houses or Brokers. In this method, the companies issues are not offered directly to the public. This method generally consists of two stages:

- The first stage of the issuing company shares is direct sale to the Issue House and Brokers at an agreed price
- The second stage, the intermediaries are resell the above shares to the ultimate investors.

The Issue Houses or Stock Brokers purchase the securities at a negotiated price and resell at a higher price. The difference arised in the purchases and sale price is known as turn or spread.

This method of sale is not common in India. It is relieved the problem of printing and advertisement of prospects and making allotment shares of the company.

Placement

The Issue Housing or Brokers buys the securities outright with intention of placing them with their clients afterwards. In this case, the brokers act as wholesalers selling it retail to the public. The Issue Houses or Brokers keep their own list of clients and contact clients for selling the securities.

Merits of the Placement

- This method is a useful method for floatation of shares
- This method is suitable for small companies to issue shares

Disadvantages of Placement

The main disadvantages of this method as outlined below:

- The securities are not widely distributed to the large section of investors
- Only a selected group of small investors are able to buy a large number of shares and get majority holding in a company
- Placement method has limited use in India.

Rights Issue

This is a method of raising funds in the market by an existing company. A right means an option to by certain securities at a certain privileged price within a certain specified period. Shares are offered to existing shareholders are called rights shares.

Rights share are offered to the existing shareholders in a particular proportion to their existing share ownership. The ratio in which the new shares or debentures are offered to the existing share capital would depend upon the requirement of capital. The rights themselves are transferable and saleable in the market.

A company issuing rights is required to send a circular to all existing shareholders. The circular must provide information on how additional funds would be used and their effect on the earning capacity of the company. The company must normally give a time limit atleast one month to two months to shareholders to exercise their right. In the case, the rights are not fully taken up, the balance is to be equitably distributed among the applicants for additional shares.

Advantages of Rights Issue

- Under this, there is no underwriting, brokerage, advertising and printing of printing of prospectus expenses. Therefore, the cost of issue is minimum
- It ensures that equitable distribution of shares to all existing shareholders. However, control of company remains undistributed as proportionate ownership in the company remains the same
- It prevents that the directors from issuing new shares in their own name or to their relatives at a lower price and get controlling right.

PLAYERS IN THE NEW ISSUE MARKET

There are many players in the new issue market. The important of them are the following:

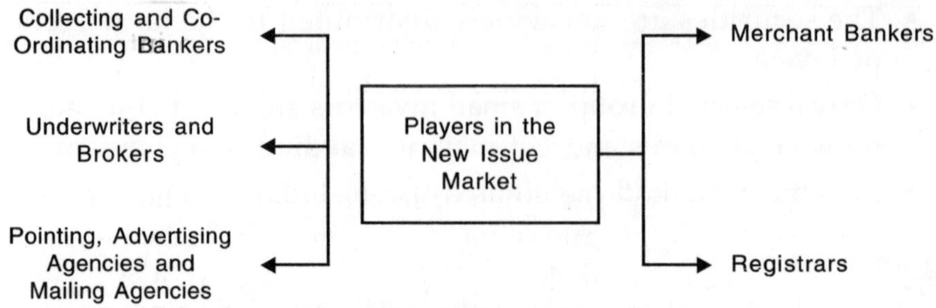

Fig. 7.2 Players in the New Issue Market

Figure 7.2 indicates the important players in the market. They are outlined as below:

- Merchant Bankers
- Registrars
- Collecting and Coordinating Bankers
- Underwriters and Brokers
- Printers, Advertising Agencies and Mailing Agencies

Merchant Bankers

According to the notification of the Ministry of Finance defines a merchant banker as "any person who is engaged in the business of issue management either by making arrangements regarding selling, buying or subscribing to the securities as manager, consultant, advisor, or rendering corporate advisory service in relation to such issue management." This definition revealed that they are the issue managers, lead managers and co-managers and are responsible to the company and SEBI.

Qualities Required of Merchant Bankers

- Merchant bankers has ability to analyse various aspects like technical, financial and economic aspects concerning the formation of an industrial project.
- Merchant bankers should have knowledge about the various aspects of capital markets trends in stock exchange, psychology of investing public, change in the economic and technological environment in the country.
- Merchant bankers has ability to buildup the bank client relationship and issue upto the clients expectations with total involvement in the project assigned to them.
- They adopt innovative approach in developing capital market instruments to satisfy the ever changing needs of investing public.

- The success of the merchant bankers depend on integrity and maintenance of high professional standards.

Registrars

Registrars are an important types of intermediaries who undertake such as collect the applications for new issues, their cheques, stock invests etc., classify and computerise them. They also allot in consultation with the regional stock exchange relating norms in the event of oversubscription and before a public representative. They are appointed by the company in consultation with the merchant bankers to the issue. Registrars have play a major role, next to merchant bankers with respect of servicing investors.

Role of Registrar in Pre-issue

The role of Registrar in the pre-issue, during the currency of issue, pre-allotment, allotment and post allotment are as outlined below:

Exhibit 7.5 Role of Registrar in Pre-issue

- Suggest draft application form to the merchant bankers.
- To help identification of the collection centers. The choice of collection centres and collecting banker is difficult to the success of the issue.
- To assist in opening collection accounts with banks and laydown procedure for operation of these accounts.
- To send instructions to collecting branches, for collection of application along with cheques, drafts, stock invest separately and remittance of funds.
- To workout modalities to receive the collection figures on a regular basis until the subscription list is closed.

During the Currency of Issue

Exhibit 7.6 During the Currency of Issue

- To receive the collection figures every day.
- To tabulate and classify the collection data on the basis of the standard proforma of slabs of shares applied for.
- To keep the merchant bankers and the company informed of the progress of total subscriptions.
- To inform the stock exchange about the closure of issue.

Pre-Allotment Work

Exhibit 7.7 Pre-Allotment Work

- To get all application forms from the collecting bankers and sortout valid and invalid application forms.
- The valid applications are to be categorised and grouped as cash, draft and stock investment applications.
- To reclassify the valid applications eligible for allotment.
- To prepare the list with inverted numbers and then approach the regional stock exchange for finalising the basis of allotment, in the event of over subscription.
- To finalise the allotment as per the basis approved by the stock exchange.
- To tally the final list approved for allotment and rejections within the house control numbers and correct mistake, if any.

Allotment Work

Allotment of shares is an important work of Registrar. The system of proportional allotment was adopted for new issues in 1993. A new quota system was approved by SEBI in April, 1995. According to the new system 50% of quota for small investors and another 50% for other categories. The small investors include all applicants upto 1000 shares.

Post Allotment Work

Exhibit 7.8 Post Allotment Work

- To get the letters of allotment and refund orders printed ready for despatch. They have to mail on or before 70 days from the closing date of subscriptions. For any delay, get the permission of the Registrar of Companies and the relevant regional stock exchange.
- To submit all statements to the company for their final approval.
- To arrange to pay the brokerage and underwriting commission and submit their relevant statements.
- To assist the company in getting the allotted shares listed on the stock exchange.

Collecting and Co-ordinating Bankers

Collecting and Co-ordinating Bankers may be the same or different. Collecting bankers collect the subscriptions in cash, cheques, stock investment etc. Co-ordinating bankers collect the information on subscriptions and co-ordinate the collection work. They monitor the work and keep inform them to the registrars and merchant bankers.

Underwriters and Brokers

These functions and role of underwriters are already discussed. Underwriters may be financial institutions, banks, mutual funds, brokers etc. and undertake to mobilise the subscriptions upto balance limits, failing to secure subscriptions as agreed to. They have to make good the shortfalls by their own subscriptions. Brokers along with their network of sub-brokers market the new issues by their own circulars, sending the application forms and follow up recommendations.

Printers, Advertising Agencies and Mailing Agencies

Printers, advertising agencies and mailing agencies are the other organisations involved in the new issue market operations.

Stock Market Intermediaries

The major players in the market are the issuers of securities, namely, companies, intermediaries like brokers, sub-brokers and the investors who bring in their savings and funds into the market.

The stock brokers are of various types, namely:

Client Brokers

They are doing simple brokering between buyers and sellers and earning only brokerage for their services from the clients.

Floor Brokers

They are authorised clerks and sub-brokers who enter the trading floor and execute orders for the clients or for members.

Jobbers

Jobbers are those members who are ready to buy and sell simultaneously in selected scrips, offering bid and offer rates for the brokers and sub-brokers on the trading floor and earning profit through the margin between buying and selling rates.

Arbitragers

Arbitragers are those who do inter market deals for a profit through differences in prices as between markets i.e., buy in Kolkata and sell in Mumbai and vice versa.

Badla Financiers

Badla financiers are those members who finance carry forward deals in specified group for a return in the form of interest, called badla rate, they lend money or shares for the brokers who are overbought or oversold respectively at the time of settlement.

SPECIAL FEATURES OF THE INDIAN CAPITAL MARKET

Exhibit 7.9 Special Features of the Indian Capital Market

- Greater reliance on debt instruments as against equity and in particular borrowing from financial institutions.
- Issue of debentures, specifically, convertible debentures with automatic or compulsory conversion into equity without the normal option given to investors.
- Floatation of Mega Issues for the purpose of take over, amalgamation etc. and avoidance of borrowing from financial institutions for the fear of their discipline and conversion clause by the bigger companies, and this has now become optional.
- Avoidance of underwriting by some companies to reduce the costs and avoid scrutiny by the FIs. It has become optional now.
- Fast growth of mutual funds and subsidiaries of banks for financial services leading to larger mobilisation of savings from the capital market.

VALUATION OF SECURITIES

Valuation of securities means professionally estimating, assessing, determining, setting the price, worth and value of a thing or an asset. As the objective of any investment is to find out an asset that is worth more than its cost, a proper understanding of the process of valuation is necessary for any real or financial investment decisions, Portfolio Selection and Management, and financing decisions. The valuation techniques which provide investors a benchmark or standard of comparison between assets and firms which have varying financial characteristic, it enables investors to appraise the relative attractiveness of assets and firms. Therefore, we shall discuss below certain value concepts, general principles of valuation, and the way in which certain specific securities can be valued.

Book Value

The book value of an asset or a organisation is based on accounting reports. In the case of a physical asset, it is equal to the asset's historical cost less accumulated depreciation. In the case of a common stock, it is equal to the net worth (paid up capital + reserves and surplus) of the firm divided by the number of outstanding shares. Its present symbolically.

Book Value of Physical Asset = Historical cost – Accumulated depreciation

Book Value of Common Stock =

$$\frac{\text{Networth (Paid up Capital+Reserve and Surplus)}}{\text{Number of Outstanding Shares}}$$

Going-concern Value

Going concern value applies to a business firm as a continuing operating unit. It is based primarily on how profitable a firm's operations would be as continuing entity i.e., the entity that is unlikely to go out of business in the foreseeable future.

Liquidation Value

The liquidation value is the value of the business organisation which has ceased or wound up its business operations, or which has gone into liquidation. The liquidation value of an ordinary share is equal to the value realised from liquidating all the assets of the firm minus the amount to be paid to all the creditors, preference shareholders, and other prior claimants by the number of outstanding ordinary shares.

Market Value

It means that the market value of an asset is simply the price at which it is traded in the market at a given point of time.

Intrinsic or Present Value

Intrinsic value is also known as a fair market value or investment value. It is also equal to the present values of a stream of cash flows expected to be generated by the asset. The technique for finding out present value is known as discounting. Market value truly reflects intrinsic value of the market is perfectly competitive.

Terminal Value

Terminal value means that the terminal value of the asset or money is the value of today's money at some point of time in future, and the method for ascertaining it is known as compounding.

Time Value of Money

It connotes that a rupee today in hand is worth more than a rupee tomorrow (or in future) because it can be invested and made to earn interest immediately, and because the present consumption is valued more than the future consumption by the people.

General Principles of Valuation

Any asset or security valuation derives its value from the cash-flows. It is expected to generate in future or tomorrow. The present value of the future or delayed payoff can be found by multiplying that payoff by the discount factor which is less than one and which can be defined as:

$$\text{Discount Factor} = \frac{1}{1+\text{Discount rate}}$$

It follows that to obtain the value of the asset we shall need to know two things.

- The expected or projected future cash flows
- The discount rate which is also known as the hurdle rate or the opportunity cost of investment. The discount rate is equal to the Required Rate of Return which is approximated by the rate of return available on the next best opportunity for investment which the investor forgoes by investing in the asset question. We shall illustrate below the basic valuation model by giving the present value formulae for only five types of future cash flows, although there is a wide range of possibilities in respect of the types of cash flows.

(i) Cash flow to be received at the end of one year

$$PV = \frac{C_1}{(1+r_1)}$$

(ii) Cash flow to be received at the end of say, fifth year

$$PV = \frac{C_5}{(1+r_5)^5}$$

(iii) Continuous uneven (not the same) stream of cash flows to be received at the end of each year for a given period of time.

$$PV = \frac{C_1}{(1+r_1)} + \frac{C_2}{(1+r_2)^2} + \frac{C_3}{(1+r_3)^3} + \ldots\ldots \frac{C_n}{(1+r_n)^n}$$

$$\text{or} \quad PV = \sum_{t=1}^{n} \frac{C_1}{(1+r_t)^t}$$

(iv) Continuous even (fixed) stream of cash flows to be received at the end of each year for a given period of time. This is known as annuity which can be valued as:

$$PV = \frac{C}{(1+r)} + \frac{C}{(1+r_2)^2} + \ldots\ldots \frac{C}{(1+r_n)^n}$$

$$\text{or} \qquad PV = \sum_{t=1}^{n} \frac{C_1}{(1+r_t)^t}$$

$$\text{or} \qquad PV = C\left[\frac{1}{r} - \frac{1}{r(1+r_t)^t}\right]$$

(v) Continuous even (fixed) stream of cash flows to be received indefinitely. This is known as perpetuity and can be valued as

$$PV = \frac{C}{r}$$

In all of the above formulae

where,

PV = Present value
C = Cash flow
t = End of the year (period)
n = Duration of cash flow
r = Discount rate

The term r_t in these equations implies that, in principle, there has to be a different discount rate for different future periods. The higher rate can be applied for the longer maturity. However, since normally a flat term structure of interest rates is assumed in the context, the term r_t can be replaced by the terms.

The level of PV of the assets depends upon the timing of the cash flow and the level of discount rate, given the discount rate, the lower the PV. Thus, the PV is inversely related to both the timing of cash flow and the discount rate. Closely related to the concept of PV is inversely related to both the timing of cash flow and the discount rate. Closely related to the concept of PV is that of net present value, which is equal to PV minus the required investment or the cash outflows (costs) associated with the investments.

The reverse process of discounting is known as compounding. Investment may be at simple interest rate or compound interest rate; in the case of the latter, each interest receipt is reinvested to earn further interest in subsequent periods; there is no such possibility in the case of former. There is a considerable difference in the growth of investment under the two schemes.

The terminal value of current investment, if compounded, can be obtained as:

$$TV = CI(I+r)^t$$

where,

TV = Terminal value

CI = Current investment

r = Rate of interest

t = Number of years for which compounding is done.

The term (I+r) is referred to as the compounding factor.

Quite often, compounding is done more frequently than annually, viz., Semi-annually or quarterly or monthly. The general compounding model in such a case in

$$TV = CI(I+r/m)^{mt}$$

where,

m = number of times compounding is done during a year;

These general principles of valuation can now be applied for the purpose of valuing certain specific securities.

Valuation of Bonds

A bond or debenture is a contractual financial instrument which obligates its issuer to pay a given some money (known as par or face or maturity value) at a contracted date (maturity date) in future, and a periodic interest payment at a fixed rate of interest (coupon rate). Bond is relatively easy to value because its coupon, principal, maturity are well specified or fixed. The level of changes (volatility) in the bond price (value) are determined by expected interest receipts, maturity, investors' required rate of return, maturity value and changes in the market (current or prevailing) interest rates. It defined as

$$PVB = \sum_{t=1}^{n} \frac{C_t}{(1+r)^t} + \frac{FV}{(1+r)^n}$$

where,

PVB = Present Value of Bond

C = Annual Interest Receipts

FV = Face Value

r = Appropriate required Rate of Return

n = Maturity Period

The Relationship between Interest Rates and Bond Prices

The relationship between interest rates and bond prices are as outlined below:

- When the coupon rate equals the Require Rate of Return the bond will sell at par; and when the coupon rate is less (greater) than the Required Rate of Return it will sell at a discount (premium).
- The price of the bond approaches its par value as its approaches maturity.
- Bond prices move inversely with interest rates changes.
- For given change in interest rates, a change in bond price will be greater, if the term to maturity will be longer i.e., the bond price volatility and the length of maturity are directly related, but the percentage change in the bond price or the degree of sensitivity of bond price to changes in interest rates increases at a diminishing rate as the term to maturity (the time remaining until maturity) increases.
- Holding maturity constant, a decrease in interest rates raises bond prices more than an equal increase in interest rates lowers them. It means that the capital gains from a decrease in interest rates will always exceed the capital losses from an equal increase in interest rates.
- The higher the coupon rate, the smaller the percentage price change due to any given change in interest rates, means that the bond price volatility and bond coupon rate are inversely related.

Valuation of Preference Shares

The valuation of preference shares (PS) is difficult in one sense, and easy in another. It is difficult because there are many types of PS. But; if we assume that PS is a perpetual security (which it basically is), its valuation becomes relatively easy. Thus, assuming that PS earns a fixed rate of return for an infinite period of time, its value can be calculated as follows:

$$PVPS = \frac{DPS}{rPs}$$

where, PVPS = Present Value of Preference Share

DPS = Dividend on PS

rPS = The required rate of return on PS

Common Stock Valuation

The valuation of common stock (CS) or ordinary shares (OS) is complex and difficult because its cash flows and maturity are not fixed. There are three well known approaches to CS valuation as outlined below:

- The efficient market approach
- The technical approach
- The fundamental approach

Efficient Market Analysis

The first one, although widely debated, is often regarded as unconvincing, improbable, and uncomfortable in practice. It appears to be preoccupied with the investor's source and manner of assessment of information. It holds that shares prices fully reflect all the relevant information that is available and usable and that they reflect the fair economic values of shares. Its practical implications are that not much time, money, energy need to be devoted to the analysis of securities, and that there is little use of employing trading or investment strategies for maximising the investment return.

Technical Analysis

This involves a methodology for forecasting fluctuations in prices of Individual Securities or portfolios of securities. It holds that changes in share prices can be detected by analysing the market activity by studying either the patterns of past price fluctuations or the movements in certain technical indicators. The underlying economic variables which affect the company and the markets are not considered important in this approach.

Fundamental Analysis

This approach believes that the price or the intrinsic value of CS is determined by certain basic economic factors or economic fundamentals. It also holds that the market price and the intrinsic value CS can differ for sometime, but they would eventually tend to be equal.

The fundamental analysis includes present value analysis and Price-Earnings (P/E) Analysis. The former primarily uses the Dividend Valuation or Dividend Capitalisation or Dividend Discount Model.

Dividend Capitalisation Model (DCM)

Since dividends are the only cash payments shareholders receive directly from the companies, they are regarded as a foundation of CS valuation. However, there are no fixed dividends and maturity period in case of CS. Therefore, usually, the following three types of assumptions regarding the flow of dividends are made in order to find out the value of shares.

- Dividends remain constant
- Dividends grow at a constant rate
- Dividends grow at a variable rate

Constant Dividends

When it is assumed that the future dividends would be equal to the current dividend, it becomes a case of perpetuity (like preference shares) and it is defined.

$$PVPS = \frac{D_o}{rCS}$$

where, PVCS = Present Value of Common Stock

Do = Current dividend expected to be received in future

rCS = Required rate of return appropriate for equity

Constant Rate of Growth of Dividends

When it is assumed that, starting with the current dividends (Do), dividends would grow it constant or normal rate of growth of over an indefinite time horizon, and that the discount rate is greater than this growth rate, the price of CS would be

$$PVCS = \frac{D_1}{rCS - g}$$

where,

D_1 = Dividend expected to be received at the end of year one.

g = Expected (constant) rate of growth of current dividend.

Variable Growth Rate of Dividends

This is third assumption is that there is a supernormal growth in dividends. For example, they grow at the rate of g_1 for the first five years and g_2 thereafter. One can assume 2003 or any number of growth rates or stages of growth. But usually, the discussion is confined to two growth rates model. Usually, it is also assumed that $g_1 7 g_2$. The price of CS can then be arrived at as follows:

$$PVCS = \frac{D_o(1+g_1)}{(1+rCS)^t} + \frac{1}{(1+rCS)^n} \times Pn$$

where,

Do = Current dividend

g_1 = Its supernormal growth rate

n = number of years of supernormal growth

Pn = Price of stock at the end of super normal growth period which is based on the dividend growth rate of g_2 from n+1 to infinite.

It has been suggested by some that the industrial life cycle framework in which the pioneering stage, maturity stage and stability stage are characterised by varying growth rates can help investors to ascertain the growth stage of the company and accordingly to form the judgement regarding the level and duration of the growth rate.

Valuation of Convertible Securities

A convertible security is a bond or a preference share that can be converted into the common stock of the same company at specified conversion terms at the option of the investor. The valuation of such security is quite complex.

In this context, it is essential to know the meaning of the following terms:

Conversion Ratio is the number of shares the investor receives on conversion of a bond. Conversion price or Exercise Price (Rate) or Strike Price (Rate) is the par value of bond divided by the conversion ratio. Conversion value at the time of issuance of bond is its conversion ratio times the market price per share. Conversion premium is the differential between the conversion value and the price at which the bond is sold or issued.

In case of valuing convertible bond, one has to remember that it is both a debt security and a common stock. It offers the purchaser a stream of interest payments and a return principle on maturity; and also the capital gain of the price of CS rises sufficiently. Every CB has a conversion option value or conversion value or the value of the common stock received upon conversion. It can be defined as:

$$CVCB_1 = \left[\sum_{q=t+1}^{m} \frac{C}{(1+r)^q}\right] + \frac{CR \times Pe_1 m}{(1+r)^{m,t}}$$

where,

CVCB = Conversion value of convertible bond

C = Periodic interest receivable till the time of conversion

m = Time of conversion

CR = Conversion ratio

Pe, m = Price per equity share at time where M is time of conversion; and r the investor's required rate of return.

QUESTIONS FOR DISCUSSION

1. Write a short notes on the following:
   (a) Capital market
   (b) Debt
   (c) Equity
   (d) Security
   (e) Primary market
   (f) Secondary market
   (g) Industrial Securities
   (h) Government Securities
   (i) Long-term Securities
   (j) Origination
   (k) Underwriting
   (l) Distributing
   (m) Public Issues
   (n) Rights Issue
   (o) Players in the new issue market
   (p) Merchant Bankers
   (q) Registrars
   (r) Collecting and Co-ordinating Bankers
   (s) Book Value
   (t) Going concern value
   (u) Intrinsic or present value
   (v) Liquidation value
   (w) Time value of

2. Discuss the capital market and its functions.
3. Explain the capital market structure.
4. Briefly describe the Industrial Securities Market.
5. Briefly explain the new issue market functions.
6. Discuss the underwriting, its functions and merits.
7. Briefly elucidate distribution and its method.
8. What are the merits and demerits of prospectus.
9. Explain the players in new issue market.
10. Who are merchant bankers? Explain the qualities of merchant bankers.
11. Discuss the Registrars and its role in capital market.
12. Discuss the stock market intermediaries.
13. What are the features of capital market?
14. How to valuation of securities?
15. Briefly note on general principles of valuation.
16. Explain the valuation of bonds.
17. Discuss the valuation of preference shares.
18. Describe the common stock valuation and its procedure.
19. Explain the valuation of convertible securities.

REFERENCES

Bhole L.M., *Financial Institutions and Markets,* Tata McGraw Hill, New Delhi, 2003.

Prasanna Chandra, *Investment Analysis and Portfolio Management,* Tata McGraw Hill, New Delhi 2003.

Van Home J., *Financial Management and Policy,* Prentice Hall of India, New Delhi

Prasanna Chandra, *Financial Management,* Tata McGraw Hill, New Delhi, 2003.

Pandey I.M., *Financial Management,* Vikas Publishing House, New Delhi, 2004.

Fischer, Jordon, *Security Analysis and Portfolio Management,* Pearson Education, New Delhi, 2003.

ICAI Study Material, *"Management Accounting and Financial Analysis."*

CHAPTER

8

PORTFOLIO MANAGEMENT

Learning Objectives

In this chapter, we shall discuss about definition of Portfolio Management, relationship between Risk and Return, Portfolio Objectives, Markowitz Portfolio selection model and its assumption and limitations, Capital Asset, Preung Preung Model assumptions limitations, Modern Portfolio theory, Portfolio investment Process, Portfolio objectives and constraints.

INTRODUCTION

"The life of every man is diary in which he means to write one story, and writes another; and his humblest hour is when he compares the volume as it is with what he vowed to make it."

— By J.M. Barrie

Definitions of Portfolio Management

The traditional investments course covers two principal topics:

- Security Analysis
- Portfolio Management

Security Analysis involves estimating the merits and demerits of individual investments.

Portfolio Management concerns the construction and maintenance of a collection of investments. The portfolio management primarily involves reducing risk rather than increasing return. Return is obviously important, though, and the ultimate objective of the portfolio manager is to achieve a chosen level of return by incurring the least possible risk.

The aim of portfolio management is to achieve the maximum return from a portfolio which has been delegated to be managed by an investment manager or financial institution. The manager has to balance the parameters which define a good investment i.e., security, liquidity and return. The goal is tc obtain the highest return for the client from the managed portfolio.

The systematic development and implementation of an investment strategy, the purpose of which is to achieve the investor's financial goals. Often portfolio management is mistaken for the simple buying of new securities and the selling of current holdings.

The process of managing assets and investments in order to achieve desired organisational outcomes which consists of the following activities:

- Selection
- Management
- Evaluation

RELATIONSHIP BETWEEN RISK AND RETURN

Risk and return have a fundamental relationship that is well known to finance students. It is illustrated in figure 8.1. The more risk someone bears, the higher the expected return. Furthermore, there is some rate of return that can be earned without bearing any risk. This is called the risk less rate of interest in finance theory.

Figure 8.1 has findout two important points:

- The risk/return relationship is based on expected return. The expected return is the weighted average of all possible returns, with the weights reflecting the likelihood of each possible return. It is not correct to say that riskier securities have higher returns, although you often hear people making this statement. If riskier securities always had higher returns, they would not be risky.
- The risk we are talking about is unavoidable nor undiversifiable risk.

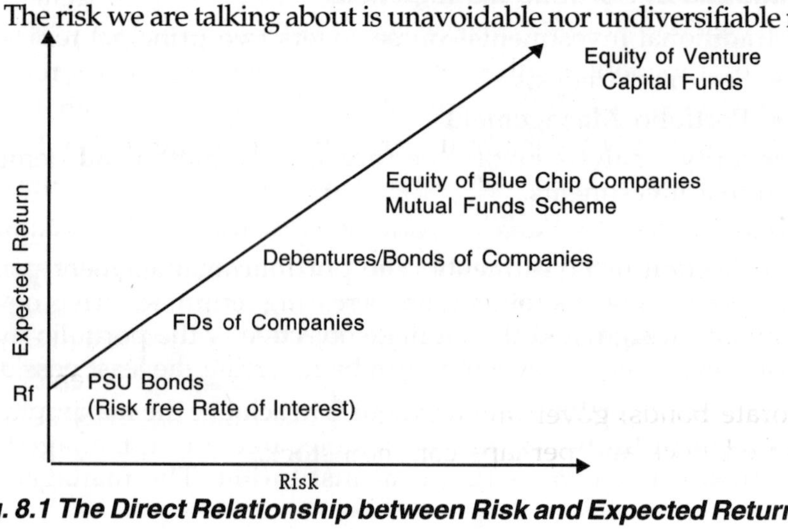

Fig. 8.1 The Direct Relationship between Risk and Expected Return

Portfolio Objectives

There are four traditional objectives. They are as outlined below:

- Stability of principal
- Income
- Growth of income
- Capital appreciation

Stability of Principal

Sometimes the beneficiary of a portfolio cannot stand any chance of loss to the original principal. This might be because of by law provisions, statute, or the client's attitude toward risk. When some one says "I don't want any chance of losing the money I invest." The fund manager should interpret this person's objective as stability of principal. This is the most conservative portfolio, and over the long run, it will generate the most modest return.

When stability of principal is the objective, the appropriative investment vehicles include any of the money market instruments and bank certificates.

Income

The income objectives differs from stability of principal in that there is no specific prescription against period declines in principal value. For instance, a new issue of five year Treasury notes might have a coupon rate of 9 per cent. If the fund manager were to buy Rs. 10,000 of these at par, they would yield Rs. 900 per year. However, these securities are marketable, and they are interest rate sensitive. If the general level of interest rates rises, the market value of these securities will fall. On paper the foundation will show a loss on these securities relative to their purchase price. If they are held until maturity, though, they will be redeemed at the original par value, and the paper loss will disappear. Had it been necessary to sell them prior to maturity, an actual realised loss certainly would have been possible.

The consequence of fluctuations in market value vary. In this instance of a fund to benefit a public non-profit organisation, an income objective is probably more reasonable than one of stability of principal when income is the chosen objective, appropriate investments include corporate bonds, government bonds, government agency securities, preferred stock and perhaps common stock.

Growth Income

The time value of money is one of the two key concepts in finance. Rupees today are worth more than an equal number of rupees at any point in the future. A growth of income objective sacrifices some current return for some purchasing power protection. This objective usually involves a reduced initial income payout, but one that grows over time and eventually overtakes the level amount from an income objective.

Funds with growth of income as the primary objective often seek to have the annual income increase by at least the rate of inflation. A growth of income objective requires some investment in equity securities.

Capital Appreciation

Occasionally it is not important that a portfolio generate any income at all. A retired couple, for example, might receive pension and social security checks that are sufficient finance their retirement life cycle. If these people have an investment portfolio, they might be more interested in having it continue to grow the value rather than in getting additional income from it.

There is also an income tax consideration. Interest or dividends received are immediately taxable. Capital gains are not taxed until they are actually realised.

MARKOWITZ PORTFOLIO SELECTION MODEL/THEORY

Harry Markowitz opened the door to modern portfolio theory. He started with the idea of risk aversion of average investors and their desire to maximise the expected return with the least risk Markowitz is a theoretical framework for analysis of risk and return and inter-relationships. He used the statistical analysis for measurement of risk and mathematical programming for selection of assets in a portfolio in an effective manner. His framework led to the concept of efficient portfolios. An efficient portfolio is expected to yield the highest return for a given level of risk or lowest risk for a given level of return.

Markowitz has generated a number of portfolios within a given amount of money or wealth and given preferences of investors for risk and return. Expenditures and investment requirements differs from individual to individual. Given the preferences, the portfolio selection is not a simple choice of any one security or securities, but a right combination of securities. He emphasised that quality of a portfolio will be different from the quality of individual assets within it.

Yield/return and reward are two components of investment considered by investors. The expected return/yield may vary depending on the assumptions. Risk index has measured by the variance or the distribution around the mean, its range etc. which are in statistical terms as known as variance and covariance. Harry M. Markowitz is credited with introducing new concepts of risk measurement and their application to selection of portfolios.

A portfolio of assets involved the selection of securities. A combination of assets or securities is known as a portfolio. Each individual investor puts his in a combination of assets which are depending on his wealth, income and preferences.

Assumptions of Markowitz Theory/Model

The Markowitz model is based on the following assumptions regarding investor behaviour.

- Investors are rational and behave in a manner as to maximise their yield utility with a given level of income or money.
- Investors have free access to accurate and current information on the returns and risk.
- The markets are efficiently and absorb the information quickly and perfectly.
- Investors are risk averse and try to minimise the least risk and maximise high return.
- Investors base decisions on expected returns and variance or standard deviation of returns only.
- For a given risk level, investors prefer high returns to lower returns.

Under these assumptions, a single asset or portfolio of assets is considered to "efficient" if no other asset or portfolio of assets offers higher expected return with the same (or lower) risk or lower risk with the same (or higher) expected return.

Markowitz Diversification

A portfolio that is invested in multiple statements whose returns are uncorrelated will have an expected simple return which is weighted average of the individual instruments returns. Its volatility will be less than the weighted average of the individual instruments volatilities. This is diversification. Diversification is the "free lunch" of finance. It means that an investor can reduce market risk simply by investing in many unrelated instruments. The risk reduction is "free" because the expected returns are not affected. The concept is after explained with the age-old saying "Don't put all your eggs in one bucket."

Diversification should not be confused with hedging, which is the taking of offsetting risks. With diversification, risks are uncorrelated. With hedging, they have negative correlations.

A common misperception is the notion that the more uncorrelated risks a portfolio is exposed to, the lower than portfolio's overall market risk will be. This is not true, if a portfolio is leveraged in order to take new risks, the net result is likely to increase in market risk. Let's consider an example that happens occasionally, in one form or another.

A salesman for a foreign exchange trading firm approaches the trustees of a pension plan and proposes that they add a currency over lay strategy to their existing portfolio of domestic stocks and bonds. The strategy will consist of an actively traded portfolio of currency forwards. Because forwards represent long/short positions, they require little or no up front investment. Accordingly, the strategy could be implemented without changing any of plan's existing investment. Accordingly, the strategy could be implemented without changing any of the plan's existing investments. That is why it is called an "overlay" strategy.

In addition to possibly generating positive returns, the salesman argues that the added exposure to currencies will have a diversifying effect on their portfolio-decreasing the portfolio's total market risk.

Is the salesman right? Will the overlay strategy reduce the portfolio's market risk? At first blush it is difficult to say. Fluctuations in the value of the overlay portfolio should have little or no correlation with returns on the existing portfolio. On the other hand, the overlay strategy introduces a new risk in addition to the portfolio's existing risks.

In fact, the salesman is wrong, far from reducing market risk, the overlay strategy will increase total market risk. The overlay strategy does diversify the portfolio's risks, but it also leverages them. The diversification effect will reduce market risk, but this will be more than offset by the leveraging effect.

Let's look at the situation in terms of eggs and baskets. Suppose you are carrying a basket of 12 eggs. To diversify your risk you might obtain a second basket and place six of the eggs in it. Now, carrying one basket in each hand, you will have reduced risk. Suppose instead, you act under a misperception that risk is reduced by simply carrying more baskets of eggs. Instead of dividing 12 eggs between two baskets, you instead offer to carry your friends basket of 12 eggs as well as your own. Now you are carrying two baskets of 12 eggs each. In financial terminology, you have leveraged your position. The net result is an increase in risk. In effect, this is what the salesman's overlay strategy will do to the pension portfolio.

For diversification to works it is not sufficient to add risks to a portfolio. Instead, where there are concentrations of risk these need to be reduced while other, unrelated risks are taken on.

The issue of how investors can use diversification to optimise their portfolios is the concern of portfolio theory.

CAPITAL ASSET PRICING MODEL

The Capital Asset Pricing Model (CAPM) was introduced by Treynor (1961), Sharpe (1964) and Lintner (1965). It extended portfolio theory to introduce the notions of systematic and specific risk. Capital asset pricing model is describing the relationship between risk and expected return that is used in the pricing of risky securities. CAPM says that expected return of a security or a portfolio equals the rate on a risk-free security plus a risk premium. If this expected return does not meet or beat the required return then the investment should not be undertaken.

Assumptions of Capital Asset Pricing Model

- This would apparently confirm the model's inference that high beta (risk) shares produce high returns and low beta (risk) shares produce low returns.
- All assets can be freely traded.
- All investors operate with the same planning horizon (usually one period).
- Investors can hold long or short positions in all assets they trade.
- Investors are indifferent between any two asset portfolios with identical means and variance (or investors have quadratic utility function/all asset returns are normal so that mean and variance characterise the distributions).
- There are no taxes or transaction losts.
- All investors have identical perceptions regarding the expected returns, volatilities and correlations of available risky investments.
- All investors are risk averse.
- The market portfolio is
  (a) Exits
  (b) Is measurable.

Implications of these assumptions are important. For example, if investors want to hold risky assets, the only risky asset they will hold in the market portfolio (which is usually assumed to be only tradeable public securities - this assumptions may be important). Further, if borrowing and lending are allowed at the same rate, then efficient set extends beyond the tendency point.

CAPM divides the risk of holding risky assets into systematic and specific risk. Systematic risk is the risk of holding the market portfolio. As the market moves, each individual asset is more less affected. To the extent that any asset participates in by such general market moves, that asset entails systematic risk. Specified risk is the risk which is unique to an individual asset. It represents the component of an assets return which is uncorrelated with general market moves.

According to CAPM, the market place compensates investors for taking systematic risk, but not for taking specific risk. This is because specific risk can be diversified away. When an investor holds the market portfolio, each individual asset in the portfolio entails specific risk, but through diversification, the investor's net exposure is just the systematic risk of the market portfolio.

Characteristic Line

A line that describes the relationship between an individual security's returns and returns on the market portfolio. The scope of this line is beta.

Beta

An index of systematic risk. It measures the sensitivity of a stock's returns to changes in returns on the market portfolio. The beta of a portfolio is simply a weighted average of the individual stock betas in the portfolio.

Limitations of the CAPM

- CAPM is not realistic in the real world
- CAPM assumes that all investors are risk averse and higher the risk, the higher is the return is not realistic in the security market.
- Investors ignore the transactions cost information costs, brokerage, taxes etc. and make decisions on the basis of single period horizon.

Modern Portfolio Theory (MPT) or Portfolio Theory

Modern Portfolio Theory was introduced by Harry Markowitz with his paper "Portfolio Selection" which appeared in the 1952 Journal of Finance. Thirty-eight years later, he shared a nobel prize with Morton Miller and William Sharpe for what has become a broad theory for portfolio selection.

Portfolio theory explores how risk averse investors construct portfolios in order to optimize expected returns for a given level of market risk. The theory qualifies the benefits of diversification. Out of a universe of risky assets, an efficient frontier of optimal portfolios can be constructed. Each portfolio on the efficient frontier offers the maximum possible expected return for a given level of risk.

Investors should hold one of the optimal portfolios on the efficient frontier and adjust their total market risk by leveraging or deliveraging that portfolio with positions in the risk free asset.

Based upon strong simplifying assumptions, a capital asset pricing model concludes that the market portfolio sets on the efficient frontier, and all investors should hold that portfolio, leveraged or deleveraged with positions in the risk free asset.

Portfolio theory provides a broad context for understanding the interactions of systematic risk and reward. It has profoundly shaped how institutional portfolios are managed, and motivated the use of passive investment management techniques. The mathematics of portfolio theory is used extensively in financial risk management and was a theoretical precursor for today's value at risk measures.

SHARPE RATIO

The sharpe ratio showed that the frontier is where the most efficient portfolios are, for a given collection of securities. The sharpe model goes further. It actually helps you find the best possible proportion of these securities to use, in a portfolio that contain cash. A number measuring the reward to-risk efficiency of an investment, used to create risk efficient portfolios.

The definition of the Sharpe Ratio is:

$$S(x) = (r_x - R_f)/\text{Std.Dev}(x)$$

where,

x is some investment

r_x is the average annual rate of return of x

R_f is the best available rate of return of a "risk-free" security (i.e., cash)

Std. Dev(x) is the standard deviation of r_x

The Sharpe model is a direct measure of reward to risk.

PORTFOLIO INVESTMENT PROCESS

Portfolio Management is a process encompassing many activities of investment in assets and securities. It is a dynamic and flexible operations. The objective of this service is to help to Investors, for selection of securities. The process of portfolio management involves a logical set of steps common to any decision in terms of

- Planning Stage
- Implementing Stage
- Monitoring and Controlling Stage

Planning Stage

Planning stage is the most important element of proper portfolio investment and speculation. Planning stage involves a careful review must be conducted of the investor's financial situation and current primary and secondary market conditions.

Exhibit 8.1 The Portfolio Investment Process

I Stage → **Planning**
- Investor Conditions
- Market Conditions
- Investment/Speculative Policies
- Strategic Asset Allocation

↓

II Stage → **Implementation**
- Rebalance Strategic Asset Allocation
- Tactical Asset Allocation
- Security Selection

↓

III Stage → **Monitoring and Controlling**
- Evaluate Statement of Investment Policy
- Evaluate Investment Performance

Exhibit 8.2 shows the portfolio planning stage are identified below:

- Investors conditions
- Market conditions
- Investor policies
- Statement of investment policy

Exhibit 8.2 Portfolio Planning Stage

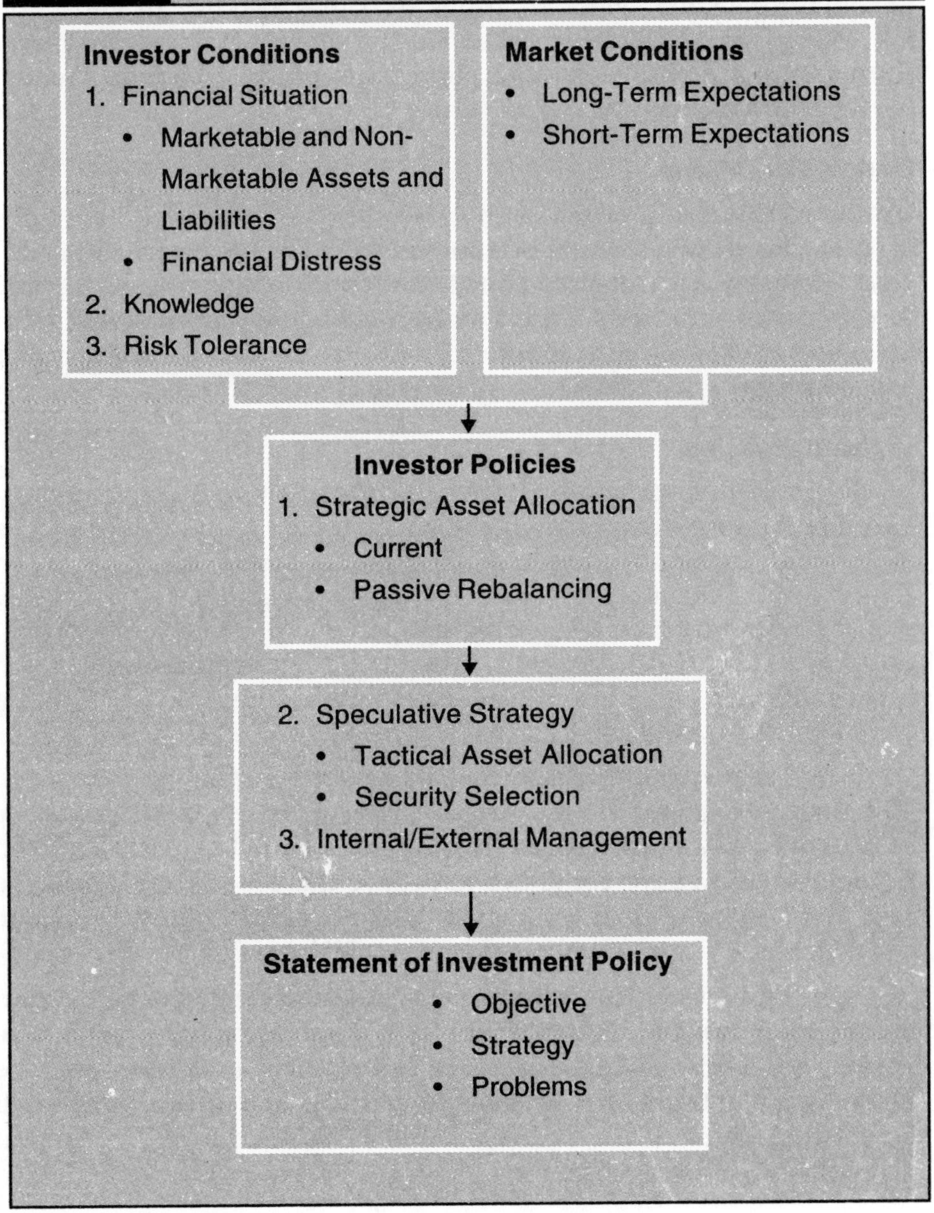

Investors Conditions

Investors conditions measures in terms of financial situation as marketable and non-marketable assets and liabilities, knowledge of the portfolio and risk tolerance of the portfolio.

This stage involves identification of investors objectives, conditions and problems of the financial situation in marketable and non-marketable assets. The investor must know financial status completely. The investor's knowledge of various securities also has an impact on the primary and secondary market. The investor must know that yearly equity returns are quite variable, short term returns on bonds. Finally, the investor considers to risk of return.

Market Conditions

Market conditions in terms of short term expectations and long term expectations. In long term expectations involved in the portfolio's tactical asset allocation will differ from the short term strategic asset allocation. In the case of short term expectations might differ considerably from longer-term expectations. Market conditions are tied to inflation and consumption of investment.

Investor Policies

Investor policies in terms of strategic asset allocation, speculative strategy and internal or external management. Investor's in portfolios makes investment decisions in terms of allocation of assets. Asset allocation refers to the percentage invested in various securities like as money market investment, Fixed income obligations, financial instruments, physical investment and financial investments. Strategic asset allocation is very different task of investors. Investors is estimated risk from the securities and portfolios of current scenario.

In the case of passive rebalancing, the investment strategies are static. They require changes as time passes, as the investor's wealth changes, as a security prices change, as the investor's knowledge expands etc. In the case of investor continues to believe that all security prices are fair, the strategic asset allocation will probably require periodic rebalancing.

After the investor has determined a current strategic asset allocation and decided how the allocation would be passively rebalanced as time passes, net worth changes, or share prices vary, a decision must be made as to the types and amounts of security speculation which will be allowed. Speculative strategy further classified as either tactical asset allocation decisions.

In the case there is no speculative strategies are to be used, the management of the portfolio is relatively easy in terms of internal and external management of the portfolios.

Implementation Stage

Implementation stage is the most important element of proper portfolio investment and speculation. Implementation stage involves a careful selection of securities investment in different sectors like as Industry, Service and Agriculture.

Exhibit 8.3 Portfolio Implementation Stage

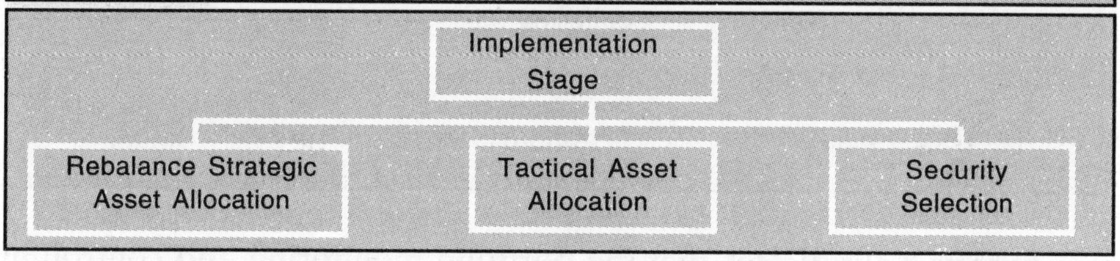

Exhibit 8.3 indicates that the portfolio implementation stage are as outlined below:

- Rebalance Strategic Asset Allocation
- Tactical Asset Allocation
- Security Selection

Rebalance Strategic Asset Allocation

Rebalance strategic asset allocation involves in terms of investors begins by periodically adjusting the asset mix to the desired mix called for in the strategic asset allocation.

Tactical Asset Allocation

If investors believes that the price levels of certain asset classes like industries or economic sectors are temporarily too high or too low, actual portfolio holdings should depart from the asset mix called for in the strategic asset allocation. Such a timing decision refers to as tactical asset allocation.

Security Selection

Security selection involves in terms of active speculation which involves the selection of securities within a given asset class, industry, or economic sector. The strategic asset allocation policy would call for broad diversification through an indexed holding of virtually all securities in the asset class.

Portfolio Monitoring and Controlling Stage

Portfolio monitoring and controlling stage is the last stage in the portfolio investment process which consists of monitoring and controlling portfolio returns in order to determine in terms of speculative decisions seem to be adding value to the portfolio and to ascertain that the portfolio's objective and constraints are being met and have not changed.

Exhibit 8.4 Porfolio Monitoring and Controlling Stage

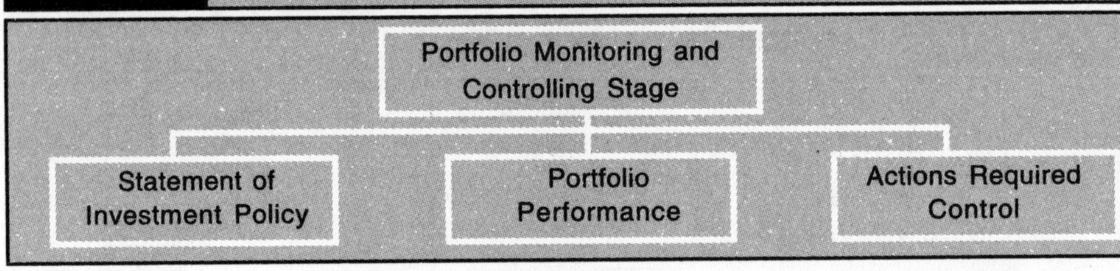

Exhibit 8.4 indicates that the portfolio monitoring and controlling stage. This stage is involved in terms of statement of investment policy, portfolio performance and actions required control.

The Statement of Investment Policy

The portfolio objective, constraints, and strategy must be stated in a written document. This written statement is known as the statement of investment policy. This statement of investment policy can be amended from time to time.

Advantages of Written Statement of Investment Policy

- A written document be prepared forces the investor to make difficult decisions which might otherwise set aside.
- A well-thoughtout statement of investment policies can add discipline and stability in the long run of management of the portfolio, reducing whipsaw reactions to temporary price swings.
- A well drafted statement of investment policies defines the investor's strategic asset allocation and passive rebalancing strategies.
- Future performance evaluation is simply impossible without a clear benchmark against which a comparison can be made.

The Portfolio Objectives

The portfolio objectives is to minimise risk and maximise return. It provides the largest pool of assets from which the owner can finance expenditures now or at some future date. The degree of risk is based on the time horizon. The portfolio will enjoy a net cash inflow or will be subject to cash withdrawals. The latter is a matter of a liquidity. Traditionally investors portfolio objectives are in terms of current income, growth in current income, capital appreciation and preservation of capital.

The Portfolio Constraints

The portfolio constraints are as identified below:

- Portfolio risk level
- Allowed security
- Diversification
- Tax and Liquidity
- Strategy
- Time horizon

Portfolio Risk Level

The portfolio objective is stated in terms of a desired rate of return, the most important problem should be the acceptable risk of the portfolio. In discipline, the risk level could be expressed as a portfolio beta or the standard deviation of portfolio returns.

Allowed Securities

All parties to the management of the portfolio should be clear understanding of the types of securities which may be purchased in terms of invested in fixed income securities, the intended duration, default risk, tax features, etc. should be clearly identified.

Diversification

Diversification is done by specify in terms of the following points:

- The minimum number of securities to be held
- The maximum percentage of the portfolio which may be held in a given security
- The maximum percentage of the portfolio which may be held in a given industry
- The variance obtained when portfolio returns are regressed against some market index.

Tax and Liquidity

Special consideration should be given to both the tax and liquidity requirements of the portfolio. Investors in a high marginal tax bracket are faced with complex portfolio decisions.

Liquidity can be obtained in two principal as below:

- By allocating an appropriate percentage of the portfolio to short term securities or money market managers
- By requiring that the bonds and equities purchased be highly marketable. In these circumstance is the more reasonable depends on why liquidity is needed.

Strategy

Finally, the statement of investment policy discuss in terms of active speculation which will be allowed. In the broad sense, speculative transactions can be related to either timing or selection.

In timing-related speculation, a given asset class is over or under weighted in comparison to the proportion called for the base line investment portfolio. In selection-related speculation, an individual security is over or underweighted in comparison to the proportion called for in the baseline investment portfolio.

Investor should know to the objectives, performance and portfolio control is essential requirement in portfolio management.

QUESTIONS FOR DISCUSSION

1. Define the following:
   - (a) Portfolio management
   - (b) Portfolio objectives
   - (c) Markowitz model
   - (d) Assumptions of Markowitz model
   - (e) Limitations of Markowitz model
   - (f) Diversification
   - (g) CAPM
   - (h) Assumptions of CAPM
   - (i) Limitations of CAPM
   - (i) Characteristic line

(k) Beta
(l) Modern Portfolio Theory
(m) Sharpe Ratio
(n) Strategic Asset allocation
(o) The statement of investment policy.

2. Discuss the relationship between risk and return.
3. Explain the portfolio objectives and its constraints.
4. Briefly describe Markowitz theory, assumptions and limitations.
5. What is Markowitz Diversification?
6. Describe the CAPM, assumptions and its limitations.
7. Briefly explain the modern portfolio theory.
8. Describe the portfolio management process.

REFERENCES

Fischer, Jordon, *Security Analysis and Portfolio Management,* Pearson Education, 2003.

Markowitz, *Portfolio Selection,* Yale University Press, Yale, 1959.

William F. Sharpe, *Portfolio Theory and Capital Markets,* McGraw Hill, U.S.A., 1970.

DyckMan, Downes and Magee, *Efficient Capital Market and Accounting: A Critical Analysis,* Prentice Hall, New Jersey, 1975.

Farrell J.J., Jr., *Guide to Portfolio Management,* McGraw Hill, New York, 1983.

Sharpe W.F., *Portfolio Theory and Capital Market,* McGraw Hill, New York, 1970.

Prasanna Chandra, *Investment Analysis and Portfolio Management,* Tata McGraw Hill, New Delhi, 2003.

■■■

CHAPTER 9

INFLATION AND INVESTMENT

Learning Objectives

- Introduction
- Meaning of Inflation
- Traditional Explanation of deflation
- Cost push inflation and demand pull inflation
- Structural factors
- Inflationary tendencies
- Inflation indicators
- Causes of inflation
- Effects of inflation
- RBI
- Role and Functions of RBI
- Monetary poling of the RBI
- Techniques /methods instruments of monetary policy
- Quantitative Techniques
- Qualitative Techniques
- Inflation on Investments
- Inflation and investment decision

INTRODUCTION

In this Chapter, we shall discuss about the inflation, traditional explanation of inflation, cost push inflation and demand pull inflation, inflationary tendencies, inflation indicators, causes of inflation, RBI role and functions, monetary policy, inflation of Investment and how helpful to investment decisions.

MEANING OF INFLATION

Inflation refers to a general and progressive increase in prices. According to Webster's New Universal Unabridged Dictionary defines the term inflation "An increase in the amount of currency in circulation, resulting in a relatively sharp and sudden fall in its value and rise in prices: It may be caused by an increase in the volume of paper money issued or of gold mined, or a relative increase in expenditures as and when the supply of goods fails to meet the demand."

This definition includes some of the basic economics of inflation and would seem to indicate that inflation is not defined as the increase in prices but as the increase in the supply of money that causes the increase in prices i.e., inflation is a cause rather than an effect.

According to the American Heritage Dictionary defines the term inflation as "A persistent increase in the level of consumer prices or a persistent decline in the purchasing power of money, caused by an increase in available currency and credit beyond proportion of available goods and services."

In this definition, inflation would appear to be the consequence or result (rising prices) rather than the cause.

Finally, inflation can be defined as a "State in which the value of money is falling as prices are rising" with the rise in prices, the real value of money in terms of number of goods or the amount of goods and services that can be purchased by one unit of currency or money will fall. Thus, if sugar price has increased over the past few years from Rs. 10 to Rs. 15 the same currency note of 100 can now buy about 6 kg of sugar, instead of 10 kg of sugar before, there in this example, here is the real loss to the consumer in terms of lowering of his purchasing power and his standard of living or consumption.

TRADITIONAL EXPLANATION OF INFLATION

According to Keynes Theory, price rise is explained as follows:

"If the resources are fully employed but the demand continues to grow, then prices will start rising. Price is a function of demand and supply and so long as there is capacity to increase supply and output to meet the demand, the prices need not rise.

According to quantity theory of money explains inflation in terms of the increase in the quantity of money. Following Fisher's equation:

$$P = M\frac{V}{T}$$

where,

P = Price

M = Money supply

V = Velocity of money

T = Total transactions

Thus, P will rise of money supply (M) or its velocity (V) will increase, with T remaining constant or not growing at the same rate. Thus; the modern Monetarist Theory also explains the phenomena of inflation in terms of the quantity of money supply.

Cost Push Inflation and Demand Pull Inflation

Cost push inflation or supply-shock inflation is a type of inflation caused by large increases in the cost of important goods or services where no suitable alternative is available. A situation that has been often cited as of this was the oil crisis of 1970s decade. It is argued that this inflation resulted from increases in the cost of oil imposed by the member states of OPEL. Since petroleum is so important to industrialised economies, a large increase in its price can lead to the increase of most products, raising the inflation rate. This can raise the normal or built in inflation rate, reflecting adaptive expectations and the price/wage spiral, so that a supply shock can have persistent effects. Monetarist economists such as Milton Friedman argue against the concept of cost-push inflation because they believe that increases in the cost of goods and services do not lead inflation without the government and its Central Bank Cooperating in increasing the money supply.

The argument is that if the money supply is constant, increases in the cost of a good or service will decrease the money available for other goods and services, and therefore the prices of some those goods will fall and offset the rise in price of those goods whose prices have increased.

The cost push factors emerge due to rise in costs of production due to wage increase or rise in profit margins. The private sector and Government sector may push up prices due to rise in input costs, namely, electricity, raw materials or wages for labour, business and industry may increases prices due to semimonopoly conditions to exploit the rise in costs of production following wage increases. Trade Union activities and recurrent wage increases have been attributed as reasons for the price rise, under this theory.

Demand pull factors arise when the total monetary demand for goods and services exceeds the available supply. This situation is caused by expanding demand, when total money exceeds required quantity. The excess demand situation for goods is the reason for inflation under this theory.

The above mentioned factors explain the rise in prices if the goods are under government controls or with administered prices, or if they are monopolistic or semimonopolistic conditions in the production of those goods.

In the case of the government administered prices in respect of coal, petrol, electricity etc. have been attributed as reasons for funneling the rise in prices of other goods. In the case of products are supplied by Multinational Corporations (MNCs), their prices are based on the principal of "what the market can bear" and not necessarily on the costs of production, under above these conditions, among others, prices of goods and services rise in a fashion of vicious circle- some price rises leading to others.

Structural Factors

In India, inflation is caused by many factors namely due to structural factors like as India is a developing economy, without full employment. There is no possibility of inflation after full employment in such an economy. Inflation happened even before full employment is reached as in the case of India due to lack of some inputs or parts, rise in their prices, inadequate supplies of some materials, labour problems and a host of other reasons.

INFLATIONARY TENDENCIES

Exhibit 9.1 Inflationary Tendencies in India

The main reasons for inflationary tendencies in India are briefly as outlined:

- Monsoon failures and inadequates agricultural products and raw materials. Cyclones and natural calamities also produce shortages leading to rise in prices.
- Trade Union activities is leading to rise in their wages beyond their productivity.
- Inadequate power supply and rise in costs of coal and power.
- Government budget deficit is leading to creation of money by RBI rising the demand pressures and leading to inflationary expectations.

Inflation Indicators

Inflation is measured in terms of the percentage rise in prices. But these prices are measured by index number with a base year, which will have price index equal to 100. These index numbers of prices measuring inflation are the following:

- Index of wholesale prices, Base year 1981-82=100
- Consumer price index for industrial workers, base year 1982=100
- Consumer price index for urban non-manual employees, base year 1984-85=100
- Consumer price index for agricultural labourers, base year 1960-61=100

All these are published on a weekly, monthly and yearly basis by the Government and RBI in their reports and publications.

CAUSES OF INFLATION

Exhibit 9.2 Causes of Inflation

The major causes of inflation:

- Railway freight charges, electricity, coal etc. rises in the administered prices of commodities under Government control.
- Deficit finance due to rise in government expenditure and fall in government revenues leading to creation of currency beyond the requirements of Trade and Industry.
- Expansion of money, supply and rise in bank credit to Government and to the private sector beyond the reasonable and to the private sector beyond the reasonable limits justified by rise in production etc.
- Supply shortages due to natural calamities, inadequate imports due to foreign exchange problems and bottleneck problems.
- Wage increases due to trade union activity, unjustified by their productivity trends.
- Rise in import prices due to rise in customs duties or higher international prices leading to higher domestic prices.
- Black marketing and hoarding by unsocial elements, traders and speculators to push up the prices and make quick profits.
- Bottleneck in transport strikes and lockouts can also create supply shortages leading to rise in prices.
- Psychological expectations of inflation may lead to rise in wage demand and to rise in prices, which in turn lead to rise in prices.
- Increase in foreign inflow of funds or rise in foreign reserves leading to rise in domestic money supply.

EFFECTS OF INFLATION

Exhibit 9.3 Effects of Inflation

The major effects of inflation:

- Inflation erodes the value of money and invisible tax, which imposed by the Government on the public. The resources wastage and unproductive expenditures of the government lead to additional burden of lower purchasing power on the public and tax payers.
- Inflation leads to social evils of hoarding, profiteering and black money.
- Fixed income people lose in real standard of living while businessmen and producers may gain from inflation.
- Social discontent and income inequalities will increase and the poor people will be more adversely affected.
- In the case of inflation is mild, it is favourable to producers to have expectations of profit and increased production of goods and services.
- In the case of inflation is mild or galloping, consumers will suffer due to fall in their real purchasing power. The quality of life will fall and saving potential will decrease.
- The inflationary results in income distribution will be unfair and discriminatory. Businessmen and traders gain more by super profits while fixed income classes, wage earners, pensioners will all suffer by fall in their real income and their standard of living.

The Reserve Bank of India

The RBI is the central bank of the country. RBI is the centre of the Indian Financial and Monetary System. As the apex institution, it has been guiding, monitoring, regulating, controlling and promoting the destiny of the Indian Financial System since its inception. It is quite young compared with such central banks as the Bank of England, Riskbank of Sweden, and the Federal Reserve Board of the US. However, it is perhaps the oldest among the central banks in the developing countries. It started functioning from April 1, 1935 on the terms of the Reserve Bank of India Act; 1934. It was a private shareholders institution till January 1949, after which it became a State owned institution under the Reserve Bank of India Act, 1948. This Act empowers the Central Government in consultation with the Governor of the Bank, to issue such directions to it as they might consider necessary in the public interest. Further, the Governor and all the Deputy Governors of the Bank are appointed by the Central Government.

The Reserve Bank of India is managed by a Central Board of Directors, Four Local Boards of Directors, and a Committee of the Central Board of Directors. The functions of the Local Boards are to advise the Central Board on matters referred to them; they are also required to perform duties has are delegated to them. The final control of the bank vests in the Central Board which consists the Governor, Four Deputy Governors, and Fifteen Directors nominated by the Central Government. The committee of the Central Board consists of the Governor, the Deputy Governors and other Directors.

Role and Functions

The preamble of the RBI Act, 1934 states that "where as it is expedient to constitute a Reserve Bank for India to regulate the issue of bank notes and the keeping of reserves with a view to securing monetary stability in India and generally to operate the currency and credit system of the country to its advantage." It described, the main role of the RBI are:

- To maintain monetary stability in the country
- To maintain financial stability and ensure sound financial institutions within the country
- To maintain stable payment system in the country
- To promote the development of financial infrastructure of markets and systems, and to enable it to operate efficiently
- To ensure that credit allocation by the financial system broadly reflects the national economic priorities and societal concerns
- To regulate the overall volume of money and credit in the economy.

The main functions are:

- Note Issuing Authority
- Government Banker
- Banker's Bank
- Supervising Authority
- Exchange Control Authority
- Promoter of the Financial System
- Regulator of Money and Credit

Note Issuing Authority

The RBI has, since its beginning, the sole right or authority or monopoly of issuing currency notes other than one rupee notes and coins, and coins of smaller denominations. The issue of currency notes is one of its basic functions. Although one rupee coins and notes, and coins of smaller denominations are issued by the Government of India, they are put into circulation only through the RBI. The Bank issues notes in the following denominations: Rs. 2, 5, 10, 20, 50, 100, 500 and 1000. The responsibility of the bank is not only to put currency into or withdraw it from circulation, but also to exchange notes as demanded by the people. The Bank can issue notes against the security of gold coins and gold bullion, foreign securities, rupee coins, Government of India Securities, and such bills of exchange and promissory notes as are eligible for purchase by the bank.

Government Banker

The RBI is the banker to the Central and State Governments. It provides to the governments all banking services like as mentioned below:

- To acceptance of deposit
- To withdrawals of funds by cheque
- To making payments as well as receipts and collection of payments on behalf of the government
- To transfer of funds
- To management of public debt.

Banker's Bank

RBI Act as Banker's Bank. Because it has a very special relationship with commercial and co-operative banks, and the major part of its business is with these banks. The RBI controls the volume of reserves of commercial banks and thereby determines the deposits/credit creating ability of the banks. The RBI hold a part or all of their reserves with the RBI. Similarly, in times of need, the banks borrow funds from the RBI. The RBI is called as the bank of last resort or the lender of last resort.

Supervising Authority

The RBI has vast powers to supervise and control commercial and co-operative banks with a view to developing an adequate and sound banking system in the country. The Reserve Bank of India has the following powers:

- To issue licence for the establishment of new banks.
- To issue licences for the setting up of bank branches.
- To prescribe minimum requirements regarding paid up capital and reserves, transfer to reserve fund, and maintenance of cash reserves and other liquid assets.

- To inspect the working of banks in India as well as abroad in respect of their organisational set up, branch expansion, mobilisation of deposits investments and credit portfolio management, credit appraisal, regionwise performance, profit planning, man power planning and training etc.
- To conduct ad hoc investigations, from time to time into complaints, irregularities, and frauds in respect of banks.
- To control methods of operations of banks so that they do not waste funds in improper investments and injudicious advances.
- To control appointment, reappointment, termination of appointment of the chairman and Chief Executive Officers of Private Sector Banks.
- To approve or force amalgamations.

Exchange Control Authority

One of the essential and important functions of the RBI is to maintain the stability of the external value of the Rupee. Its domestic policies and the regulation of the Foreign Exchange market. The task of the RBI concerned with exchange control as below:

- To administer the Foreign Exchange Control.
- To choose the exchange rate system and fix or manage the exchange rate between the rupee and other currencies.
- To manage exchange reserves.
- To interact or negotiate with the monetary authorities of the Sterling Area, Asian Clearing Union, and other countries, and with international financial institutions like IMF, World Bank and Asian Development Bank.

Promoter of the Financial System

The RBI has been rendering 'developmental' or 'promotional' services that have strengthened the country's banking and financial structure. This has helped mobilising savings and directing credit flows to desired channels, thereby helping to achieve the objective of economic development with social justice. It has helped in deepening and widening the financial system. The RBI promotion role is to preserve and enhance the stability of banking and financial system. The RBI helps to create and maintain a stable, efficient, and well functioning financial system in India.

Regulator of Money and Credit

The function of formulating and conducting monetary policy is the superior and most importance for any Central Bank. Monetary policy refers to the use of techniques of monetary control at the disposal of the central bank for achieving certain goals and objectives.

Monetary Policy of the RBI

Monetary policy in India are to accelerate economic development in an environment of reasonable price stability, and to develop appropriate institutional set up to and this process. By influencing the cost, volume, and direction of credit, monetary policy has been encouraging sectoral and overall development and supporting programmes aimed at Social Justice. It said to be controlled expansion of bank credit and money supply, with special attention to seasonal requirement of the credit.

Techniques/Methods/Instruments of Monetary Policy

Techniques/methods/instruments of monetary policy may be broadly divided into:

- General (Quantitative) Methods/Techniques
- Selective (Qualitative) Methods/Techniques

Quantitative Techniques

Quantitative Techniques are as below:

- The Bank rate
- Open market operations
- Variable reserve requirements

Bank Rate

The Bank rate is also known as the Discount Rate. It is the oldest instrument of monetary policy. According to traditional definition of bank rate is that it is rate at which the Central Bank discounts, or more accurately rediscounts-eligible bills. However, today, the term bank rate is used in a broader sense and refers to the minimum rate at which the central bank provides financial accommodation to Commercial Banks in the discharge of its function as the lender the last resort.

An increase in the bank rate means an increase in the interest rate charged by the Central Bank on its advances to commercial banks. Hence, an increase in the bank rate compels commercial banks to raise the rate of interest they charge on their loans and advances to their customers and vice versa.

An increase in the Bank Rate implies an increase in the cost of credit and vice versa. An increases in the bank rate reduces the extent of borrowings from the money market, the level of inventory holding, investment, employment and prices.

Open Market Operation

Open market operations refer broadly to the purchase and sale by the Central Bank of a variety of assets like foreign exchange, gold, government securities and even company shares in India.

Under the open market operations, the Central Bank seeks to influence the economy either by increasing the supply of money or by decreasing the money supply.

To increase the money supply, the Central Bank buys securities from commercial banks and public.

Variable Cash Reserve Ratios

The present banking system is called a "Fractional reserve banking system" because the banks need to keep only a fraction of their deposit liabilities in the form of liquid cash. The RBI has become an important and effective tool for directly regulating the lending capacity of banks. The RBI has been using two ratios:

- The Cash Reserve Ratio (CRR)
- Statutory Liquidity Ratio (SLR)

The Cash Reserve Ratio

The CRR refers to a cash which banks have to maintain with the RBI as a certain percentage of their demand and time liabilities. The Reserve Bank of India is empowered to vary the cash reserve ratio between 3 per cent and 15 per cent of the total demand and time liabilities. To facilitate the flexible operation of this system, the RBI has also been vested with the power to require the scheduled banks to maintain with it additional cash reserves, computed with reference to the excess of their total demand and time liabilities over the level of such liabilities on the base date to notified by the Reserve Bank, subject to the provision that the total reserves to be maintained with the Bank should not exceed 15 per cent of their demand and time liabilities.

Statutory Liquidity Ratio

The statutory liquidity ratio enables to impose secondary and supplementary reserve requirements, on the banking system. There are three objectives behind the use of SLR:

- To restrict expansion of bank credit.
- To augment banks investment in government securities.
- To ensure solvency of banks.

Qualitative Techniques/Selective Credit Controls

This is the most actively used technique in India. Selective credit controls seek to change the composition of credit. They are used to reduce the supply of credit in certain directions and to encourage it in desired directions. They have been used particularly to prevent speculative hoarding of sensitive commodities such as paddy, rice, wheat, pulses, oilseeds, oils and vanaspati, cotton, and sugar.

The RBI uses SCCs normally in three forms:

- Fixation of margin requirements
- Fixation of separate minimum lending rates on credit covered by selective credit controls
- Fixation of ceiling an ex-ante flows of credit.

Inflation on Investments

Investment management has to take into account of inflation on the following factors:

- Real sales or return on investments after adjustment for inflation have to be taken into account.
- Adjustments for cost over runs and project failures have to be considered before making investments in new projects.
- Projects dependent on inputs or imports whose prices are rising will have adverse effects on their profitability. Projects are to be judged through inflation adjusted returns.
- Inflation accounting of the balance sheets of companies, their cash flows inventories and their earnings and projects will have to be done by investors before making investment decisions.
- In fast rising inflationary situations, companies will be discouraged to make large scale investments due to uncertainty of cost factors and high risk factors. But mild inflation is conducive to growth of investment in good profit expectations.

- Investors do have risk-return calculations, after adjusting for inflation expectations in the economy.

Inflation and Investment Decisions

Investment decisions are affected by inflation as investors in real returns after adjusting for inflation. The adjustment is to done by taking the returns, dividends and capital gains and deflate them by an appropriate price index-wholesale price index or retail price index (consumer price index numbers). The deflation can also be done by the calculated inflation rate and arrive at the real rate of return. Such real rates are to be compared for various attractive investments before making investment decision.

QUESTIONS FOR DISCUSSIONS

1. Write a short notes on the following:
   (a) Inflation
   (b) Cost push inflation
   (c) Demand pull inflation
   (d) RBI
   (e) Note issuing authority
   (f) Government Banker
   (g) Bankers Bank
   (h) Monetary Policy of the RBI
   (i) Quantitative Techniques
   (j) Qualitative Techniques
   (k) Bank Rate
   (l) Open market operations
   (m) CRR
   (n) SLR
2. Discuss the inflation.
3. Briefly explain the cost push inflation and demand pull inflation.
4. Briefly elaborate the inflationary tendencies.
5. Explain the causes of inflation.
6. Discuss the effects of the inflation.
7. Explain the role and functions of RBI.
8. Discuss the role of quantitative and qualitative factors.

REFERENCES

Bhole L.M., *Financial Institutions and Markets*, Tata McGraw Hill, New Delhi, 2003

Bhole L.M., *Investment, Interest, and Monetary Policy in India*, Bombay University, 1974

RBI Bulletin

■■■